The Golden Book of
THE RENAISSANCE

The Golden Book of THE

RENAISSANCE

Adapted for young readers
by IRWIN SHAPIRO

from *The Horizon Book of the Renaissance*
by the Editors of *Horizon Magazine*

and J. H. Plumb
Morris Bishop
Garrett Mattingly
Kenneth Clark
Ralph Roeder
J. Bronowski
Iris Origo
H. E. Trevor-Roper
Denis Mack Smith
Maria Bellonci

GOLDEN PRESS · NEW YORK

Grateful acknowledgment is made for permission to quote from the following works:

Michelangelo: A Record of His Life, translated and edited by Robert W. Carden, Constable & Co., London, 1913. *The Notebooks of Leonardo da Vinci,* translated and edited by Edward MacCurdy, Jonathan Cape Ltd., London; Harcourt Brace & World, Inc., New York (by permission of Mrs. S. W. A. McCurdy). *The Venetian Republic* by William Hazlitt, A. & C. Black, London, 1915. *The*

Portable Renaissance Reader, edited by James Bruce Ross and Mary Martin McLaughlin, The Viking Press, Inc., New York, 1958 (from "The Dignity of Man" by Giovanni Pico della Mirandola, translated by M. M. M., and "Self-Portrait of a Universal Man" by Leon Battista Alberti, translated by J.B.R.). *The Book of The Courtier,* by Baldassare Castiglione, copyright © 1959 by Charles S. Singleton and Edgar de N. Mayhew, Doubleday & Company, Inc., New York. *Galateo* by Giovanni della Casa, translated by R. S. Pine-Coffin, Penguin Books, 1958.

U.S. copyright is not claimed for color plates on pages 10–11, 38 (top and bottom), 51, 63

Library of Congress Catalog Card Number 62-15852

CONTENTS

THE GREAT
AWAKENING

"I go to awake the dead!" said Ciriaco de' Pizzicolli.

An Italian from the town of Ancona, Ciriaco was a lover of old things, of antiquities, especially those from ancient Greece. He loved to handle old coins, to collect old manuscripts and vases and statues, to examine old temples and copy the inscriptions. During the first half of the fifteenth century he traveled in Greece, the Aegean Islands, Syria, and Egypt. Wherever he went, he put down in his diaries what he saw and thought.

The ancient Greeks had been long dead, and for a time they were all but forgotten. And so, when Ciriaco set out on his travels to

The cathedral in Orvieto, built more than a century before the Renaissance, shows the Gothic and Byzantine styles that marked the art of the Middle Ages.

discover what remained of their world, he said, "I go to awake the dead!"

Not that the ancients, of both Greece and Rome, had ever been entirely forgotten. Every educated man knew Latin, and there were always some scholars who studied the old writings. And yet, during many of the years that would become known as the Middle Ages, men seemed to have lost interest in the past. Scattered over Europe were reminders of the great days of the Roman Empire—scraps of walls, ruins of arenas, temples, and triumphal arches. To the people of the Middle Ages, they brought no dreams of glory. The ruins were a terrible warning of the wickedness that God had punished. They proved that the life of man was short, that God was almighty, and that the ways of God were mysterious and unknown.

In the city of Rome itself, the once splendid roads built by the ancients were overrun with grass and weeds. The Forum was no longer a busy marketplace, where open-air trials were held and politicians in togas made speeches to cheering crowds. Instead, it had been turned into a cow pasture. It was also a kind of stone quarry. Slabs of marble from its broken buildings and toppled columns were hauled off and used for churches and palaces.

No, for the majority of men in the Middle Ages, the past meant little; the future meant reward in heaven or punishment in hell. And between the past and the future was the harsh present, in which they were peasants working the land. Ruling them were the feudal lords who made war, protected them from other lords, and grew fat on their labor. Ruling them, too, were the priests and monks who taught them their religion, emphasizing that their lives would pass as swiftly as the crops they harvested.

They lived in a society held together and controlled by feudal law and the Catholic Church. Each man was born to his place, with his rights and duties laid down by law and custom. No one, not even the most bloodstained lord, questioned the value of religion, though men often turned from religion for the sake of power or wealth. Altogether, especially for the peasants, life was simple and primitive, and marked by war, famine, and plagues.

This society of lords, priests, and peasants was meant to last until the end of time, unchanging and unchangeable. And yet it did change. For, even in the darkest days of the Middle Ages, there was trade. Trade brought Christian merchants in touch with Moslems and Jews. It kept them from being completely cut off from the rest of the world, as if marooned on an island. It made towns grow, and sometimes created them.

Nor was trade the only reason for change. As war became more highly technical, it became more costly. As kingdoms grew in strength, kings needed more money to manage their kingdoms. As a network of churches and monasteries spread over Europe, the Church found its expenses increasing. The result was that merchants became bankers and moneylenders. Lending money to popes, emperors, and kings was a risky business. Too often the borrowers could not or would not pay back their loans. Even so, some moneylenders made huge fortunes, and this, too, helped to change the society of lords, priests, and peasants.

Men began to think less of death and more of life. They were less concerned with their future in heaven or hell, and more with their present on earth. And, curiously, because they were more concerned with the present, they tried to learn from the past, from the ancient Greeks and Romans. "I go to awake the dead!" said Ciriaco de' Pizzicolli. Indeed, it was as if the dead were being awakened and forced to give up their secrets of art and architecture and philosophy. But, even more important, the living were awakening, too, awakening from the long sleep and dark dreams of the Middle Ages. So great was the awakening that it seemed as if all mankind was being reborn. This period became known as the Renaissance, taking its name from a French word meaning rebirth.

This change, this awakening, this rebirth, did not happen suddenly. No one can say exactly when the Middle Ages ended and the Renaissance began. Historians generally agree that the Renaissance began around 1350 and lasted for about two hundred years. Petrarch, the scholar and poet who is sometimes called the first Renaissance man, was born in 1304. Boccaccio, another early Renaissance writer, was born in 1313.

Trade with foreign lands did much to change the society of the Middle Ages.
An early traveler was Marco Polo, shown here setting out from Venice in 1271.

No matter when it began, the Renaissance was an age of adventure and action, of discovery and rediscovery, of exploration and examination. During this age America was discovered, opening up a new world for settlement. Movable type was invented, opening up a new world of books for study and enjoyment. While daring navigators explored new lands, painters and sculptors explored new ways of art. Men grew interested in everything on earth. They delighted as much

in the wonders of nature as in the wonders of the past, and in the sights and sounds of the world around them.

Petrarch, for example, has been called the world's first tourist, traveling for nothing but pleasure. While in France he climbed Mont Ventoux, six thousand feet high, to see the view from the top. In a high pasture he met an old shepherd, who warned him not to make the climb. The shepherd said that he himself had climbed to the top fifty years ago,

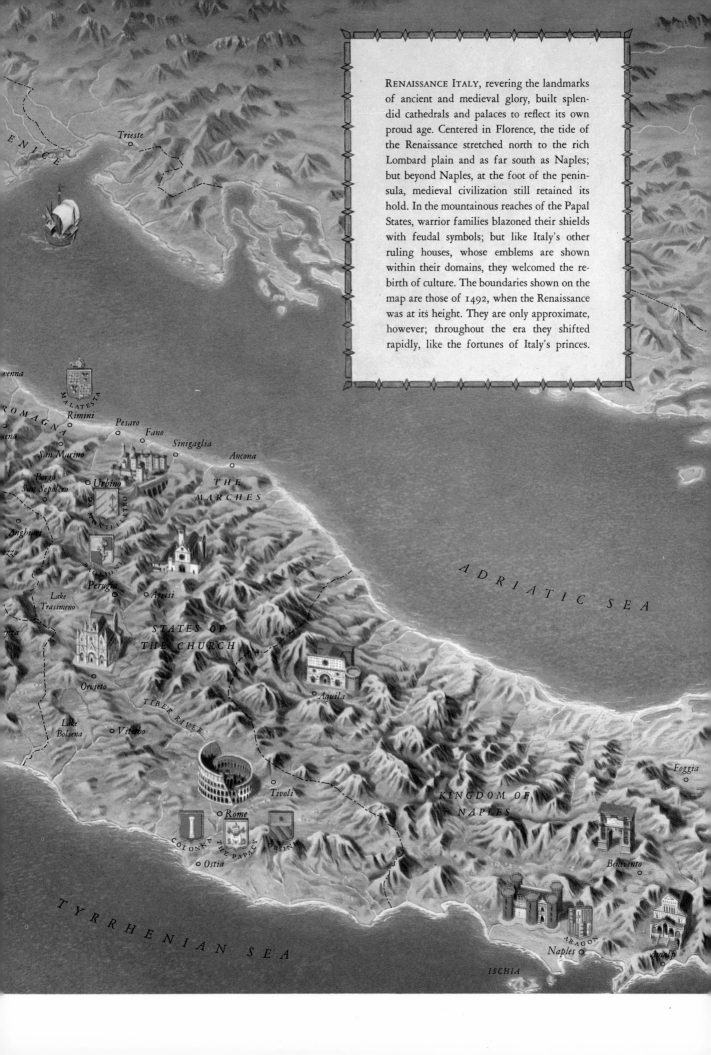

RENAISSANCE ITALY, revering the landmarks of ancient and medieval glory, built splendid cathedrals and palaces to reflect its own proud age. Centered in Florence, the tide of the Renaissance stretched north to the rich Lombard plain and as far south as Naples; but beyond Naples, at the foot of the peninsula, medieval civilization still retained its hold. In the mountainous reaches of the Papal States, warrior families blazoned their shields with feudal symbols; but like Italy's other ruling houses, whose emblems are shown within their domains, they welcomed the rebirth of culture. The boundaries shown on the map are those of 1492, when the Renaissance was at its height. They are only approximate, however; throughout the era they shifted rapidly, like the fortunes of Italy's princes.

VENICE

Trieste

Ravenna

ROMAGNA

MALATESTA

Rimini

Cesena

Pesaro

Fano

Sinigaglia

San Marino

Borgo San Sepolcro

Urbino

THE MARCHES

Ancona

Anghiari

Arezzo

MONTEFELTRO

BAGLIONI

Perugia

Assisi

Lake Trasimeno

STATES OF THE CHURCH

Siena

Orvieto

TIBER RIVER

ADRIATIC SEA

Lake Bolsena

Viterbo

Aquila

Foggia

Rome

Tivoli

KINGDOM OF NAPLES

COLONNA

THE PAPACY

ORSINI

Benevento

Ostia

ARAGON

TYRRHENIAN SEA

Naples

Amalfi

ISCHIA

and had got nothing from it except toil and repentance and torn clothes. Petrarch did not allow the words of the shepherd to stop him. He went on to the top of the mountain, where he was rewarded with the view that lay before him—the Alps, the mountains around Lyons, the river Rhone, the Bay of Marseilles. In the same way did Renaissance man climb the heights of human experience, to be rewarded by a broader view of the world.

Although the Renaissance spread to France, to Spain, to England, to the Netherlands, it began in Italy. One of the reasons was that, in Italy, independent cities, not states or kings, were the ruling powers of the land. The city-states won their independence by playing off the two greatest powers in Europe of the Middle Ages, the Pope and the Germanic Emperor, known as the Holy Roman Emperor. The Pope was supposed to rule men's souls, the Emperor their bodies. At least, that was the theory. In fact, however, the Church had property and riches which no king or emperor could match. Bishops were princes as well as bishops. The great struggle between the Empire and the Papacy was over land, money, and power.

Behind the Papacy stood the clergy—cardinals, bishops, priests, monks, and friars. They were strong in number, in learning, and in the authority of the Church. The chief strength of the Emperor came from his lands and rights in Germany, Austria, and the Netherlands. He was also King of Lombardy, with important and valuable lands in northern Italy. But he seldom visited these lands, and his enemies there grew even stronger.

The Papacy did not hesitate to encourage revolt against the Emperor. In town and village and countryside there was war between the Pope's party, the Guelphs, and the Emperor's party, the Ghibellines. The members of the two parties were foes in every way.

The Guelphs wore red roses, the Ghibellines white. The Guelphs cut their fruit in one direction, the Ghibellines in another. The Guelphs built battlements in the shape of rectangles; those of the Ghibellines were swallow-tailed. The Ghibellines of Milan even tore down the statue of Christ from the altar in the Cathedral of Crema because His face was turned to His shoulder in the manner of a Guelph.

From 1350 to 1450 Italy scarcely knew a month of peace. Yet during this time the towns grew. A few were large, like Florence, which had 100,000 people and was a center of trade and manufacturing. Many were smaller market towns of farmers, shopkeepers, and craftsmen, like Orvieto, which had a population of about 20,000. Large or small, each developed a new kind of government in the midst of feudalism. Within these cities the guilds became powerful. They were organizations of merchants and craftsmen, formed to protect their members. The guilds set prices, working conditions, and standards of work. They represented not only the richest men of the city, but also the families which knew how to rule.

Although the guilds made for a limited kind of democracy, the real basis of government was force. Long before the struggle between the Guelphs and the Ghibellines, the nobility of the cities and the surrounding countrysides had been divided by feuds and rivalries. But the guilds often needed the skill and training of the nobility in both diplomacy and war. The governments of the cities were very loose, with no constitution or written laws. All this made it easy for wealthy merchants or nobles to become the real leaders. It led to tyranny by a family or group of men, and to the powerful Renaissance princes.

To make tyranny even easier, a great bubonic plague struck Italy in the middle of

This miniature depicts the horrors of tyranny—hanging, burning, torture, and an execution.

the fourteenth century. Thousands of men and women died of the "Black Death." There were so many dead that burying them became a problem. A citizen of Siena wrote that "trenches were dug, very broad and deep, and into these the bodies were thrown, and covered with a little earth; and thus layer after layer until the trench was full; and then another trench begun. And I . . . with my own hands buried five of my children in a single trench; and many others did the like. And many dead were so ill covered that the dogs dug them up and ate them. . . . And no bells rang, and nobody wept no matter what his loss, because almost everyone expected death. . . . And people said and believed, 'This is the end of the world.'" Trade dropped, poverty was widespread, and men who wanted power knew how to take advantage of what was happening.

Yet plague or no plague, conditions in Italy were right for tyranny. From their

Political rivalry was often settled by assassination.

earliest days, the cities had been governed by force. Larger cities swallowed up smaller ones, growing by war. Italy had no central government to rule the land. The Pope might have made peace, but in 1309 the Papacy moved to the city of Avignon, in France, and it remained there until 1378. The Emperor had no control over his lands in Lombardy. So war went on, and men were constantly marching out to do battle with their neighbors.

Murder, treason, plotting, and trickery became common. Men murdered their wives, wives poisoned their husbands, brother slaughtered brother, family fought family, city sacked city. In 1402 the chief members of the ruling family of Lodi were burned alive in the public square. At Bologna in 1445, the people hunted down the enemies of their favorite family and nailed their steaming hearts to the doors of a palace.

Gradually, as power was held by fewer men and wars grew less, the great city-states developed. Florence battered down Pisa and Pistoia; Venice took over Padua and Verona; Milan ate up Pavia and Lodi.

Such city-states were too large and too rich to depend on armies of ordinary citizens. They had done well enough in earlier times when the enemy was only a day's march away, but now they had to cover more ground. Also, war was becoming too technical for simple peasants and workers. The cities needed and could afford to hire the professional soldiers— the condottieri—who roamed Italy.

As the clever Venetians realized, the condottieri kept armed power from being placed in the hands of any one citizen or group. So it became a rule in Venice that no born Venetian could command its army. At first the condottieri were foreigners, like the Englishman, John Hawkwood, who led a famous band known as the White Company. Soon the tyrants of small states put themselves and their citizens out for hire. Some kept their states and their heads; others won new lands for themselves; most died violently—executed, murdered, or killed in battle.

The condottieri fought for pay, not patriotism. Their loyalty usually belonged to the highest bidder. If they were successful, they risked the jealousy of their employer. If they failed, they were dismissed or sometimes executed. One who managed to live out his life was Bartolommeo Colleoni, yet even his career was full of ups and downs. In 1458, as commander of the Venetian armies, he was welcomed to Venice by a fleet of gondolas. Only a few years earlier he had been under sentence of death for treason, and barely escaped capture.

Fighting for or against his Venetian homeland, Colleoni was as ambitious as any condottiere, and as treacherous as most. He

14

Bartolommeo Colleoni, a famous condottiere, left this statue of himself to the citizens of Venice.

worked his way up through the ranks, receiving his first command under a professional soldier in the pay of the Queen of Naples. Once Venice captured his family and held them as hostages. At other times, Venice paid his salary with castles and then stole them back. Rival condottieri swore they would drink his blood if they caught him. Colleoni may not have been the greatest soldier of his day, but he did win some important victories. As a result, he gained respect and a small state to govern in his old age. He welcomed royalty, artists, and philosophers to his castle, and even wrote a book on the art of war. He left his fortune to Venice, provided that a statue was made in his memory and placed in the square of St. Mark's. It is this monument, which still stands in the Campo Santi Giovanni e Paolo, that has kept his memory alive.

The employers of the condottiere knew that bought troops meant treacherous troops, and that they could not be trusted. There was always the danger that a condottiere would turn against the state that hired him. To avoid this danger, the Venetians and the Florentines planted spies in the camps of their condottieri. Although the use of hired professional armies increased treachery, it reduced violence. No condottiere wished to waste his fighting men. Battles became rare and sieges went on for months.

Diplomacy as we know it—the collecting of information about foreign states and carrying on negotiations with them—also arose in Italy of the Renaissance. It grew strong in the fifteenth century, when the three great city-states of northern Italy—Milan, Venice, and Florence—were almost equally powerful. The merchants of those places had already learned to use diplomacy in business. They knew how to drive a hard bargain, how to negotiate, how to form partnerships to destroy a rival. The collecting of information on people and situations was part of the stock in trade of bankers. It was not hard to do for the state what was already being done for business.

Spying, too, was widely practiced. Every Venetian who went to a foreign state was expected to spy for his country. Spying went on at home as well as abroad; it was just as important for rulers to have information about their own people. Citizens were encouraged to spy on and betray their own neighbors.

Violence was part of everyday life, and political questions were often decided by poison or the dagger. The town of Perugia was particularly unfortunate. The leading families with their armed ruffians stormed and slaughtered in the streets and churches. Those that remained alive plotted revenge, so that there seemed to be no end to the bloodshed. In 1488 the Baglioni family and their enemies, the Oddi, fought a pitched battle in the Piazza, and the governors of the city were helpless to stop it. In 1491 the Baglioni strung up 130 men, supporters of their enemies, who had found their way into the city. Shortly after this the Baglioni were saved only by the bravery and skill of Simonetto, a boy of eighteen. He held a narrow street with a few followers until they were nearly hacked to pieces. Then came the great betrayal in which four of the Baglioni were murdered in their beds—including Simonetto. Between 1520 and 1535 practically all who were left of the Baglioni were either executed or murdered.

With death always so close, men became superstitious. They turned to astrologers and magicians to help them face the uncertain future. Even the popes felt stronger in their religious faith when the signs given by the stars were favorable. Julius II fixed the date of his coronation on the advice of his astrologers, and Paul III arranged his consistories—meetings of the cardinals—according to the stars.

The sense of death and danger all about made men eager to taste the good things in life. Those in power denied themselves no delights or enjoyments. And in seeking pleasure, as in seeking power, the popes were second to none. The men of the Renaissance lived in a dangerous, exciting world. Success was all that mattered; whether it was won by good or evil was not important. But, of course, only a few princes, nobles, and merchants held power in any state. Most of the people lived as best they could. They had nothing to do with ruling, and what happened to the government troubled them only when they were defeated in battle.

Yet it would be wrong to say that the tyrants of Italy were interested only in getting power by the most cruel methods. Many of them were intelligent; some were sensitive; all wanted fame. They wanted to be known, and they wanted to be remembered. They proved their greatness by public show—by buildings, statues, paintings, pageants, tourneys, and even works of charity. They enjoyed the delights of the mind as well as those of the body, and their wealth made it possible for them to satisfy their wishes. Rich food, gorgeous clothing, delicate jewelry, masterpieces of craftsmanship, all helped the tyrants forget strain and worry. So did the reminders of the past, the ancient statues, coins, and medallions dug up from the earth.

The tyrants collected old manuscripts, and new books from the printing presses. They collected living things, too—strange animals and misshapen men. And they collected men of great ability, men who were painters or sculptors or poets or philosophers.

There was Lodovico Gonzaga, for instance, who lived from 1414 to 1478. The Gonzaga family ruled over Mantua, one of the smaller city-states. To keep from being swallowed up by the larger states, they hired out as condot-

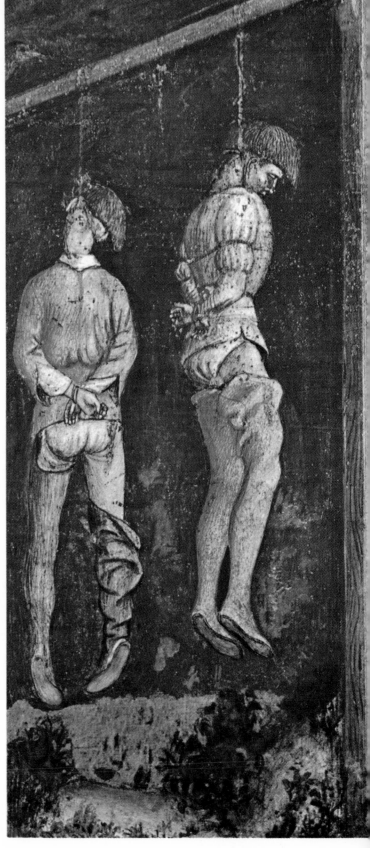

When the artist Antonio Pisanello painted these hanged and decaying corpses, he was depicting a sight common everywhere in Renaissance Italy.

tieri to Venice. From time to time they also hired out to Milan, the rival of Venice. This allowed them to be independent.

The Gonzaga fought well, and they governed as well as they fought. The population of Mantua grew to 40,000 or more, and it did a good trade in wool and silks. The Gonzaga became wealthy from war and trade. Like other princes, they spent large sums of money on pageants and public display. But they also spent money on education. Lodovico's father put his children's education in the hands of Vittorino da Feltre, whose ideas would influence European education for centuries.

Vittorino believed that education should concern itself with the body no less than with

Lodovico proved to be one of his best pupils. He became a man of action, skillful in war and diplomacy, yet with something of the scholar about him. He hired Andrea Mantegna as his court painter. Mantegna did a series of pictures that remain one of the treasures of Italy. Lodovico's taste was as good in architecture as it was in painting. He hired Leon Batista Alberti, a leading architect, to design his churches. He asked Mantuans to give money generously so that the church of Sant' Andrea "from its vast size and noble simplicity should be superior to any building of the kind in the leading cities of Italy, and worthy to stand beside the magnificence of Rome itself."

It was usual enough for Renaissance princes to build churches and palaces, and to hire painters. But Lodovico went beyond that. He encouraged poets and scholars to stay at his court. He loved books, and authorized one of the earliest printing presses in Mantua. Besides the classics, he collected manuscripts of the best Italian writers and had them illustrated by gifted craftsmen.

Lodovico set up hospitals to fight the epidemics of plague, built bridges to span the marshes surrounding the city, reformed laws and ruled justly—something rare in those days. When he died, his family was well established and well loved.

If the Gonzaga princes were loved and respected, there were others who were not. Off to the southeast of Mantua, in Rimini, ruled the most hated and feared tyrants in Italy. They were members of the Malatesta family, whose very name meant "Evil-heads." They first came to Rimini in 1216, and by the

the mind. His pupils spent part of the day wrestling, fencing, swimming, and riding. The rest of the day they studied the classic writers, such as Virgil and Homer. Vittorino was a pious Christian, and he saw to it that his pupils practiced their religion. At the same time he encouraged them to believe that individual greatness was part of man's nature.

19

Lodovico Gonzaga welcomes home his second son, Francesco, who has just been made a cardinal in Rome.

end of the century were in complete control of the town. Their history was filled with bloody tales of tragedy and brutality, but the worst tales were told of Sigismondo Pandolfo Malatesta.

At the age of fifteen, Sigismondo was already known for his skill as a soldier and his headstrong bravery. During all the years of his long rule, his people suffered hardship and war. An active condottiere, Sigismondo was continually fighting for one state or another. His treachery earned him the enmity of nearly all who employed him. Pope Pius II, with whom he feuded over land holdings, said, "Of all men who ever lived or will live, [Sigismondo] was the worst scoundrel, the disgrace of Italy. . . ." He was said to have murdered his first two wives, to have committed a number of other murders, and to have been guilty of the worst crimes known to man.

Pope Pius excommunicated him, and a few years later a council of cardinals sentenced him to burn as a heretic. When they could not capture him, they burned his effigy. Sigismondo only laughed. The Church defeated him, however, in 1463, and he was forced to give up most of his lands and power. Few people were sorry when he died in 1468.

And yet this scoundrel had had a deep knowledge of and respect for ancient philosophy. His closest friends had been scholars and artists. Among them was Alberti, the architect. Sigismondo had Alberti transform the church of San Francesco in Rimini into a Roman temple. Within it were tombs for all the Malatesta family; Sigismondo's own was carved with horns. Pope Pius said that the building seemed "less a Christian sanctuary than a temple of heathen devil-worshippers."

Even so, it was an important piece of architecture, and it remains a monument to the scoundrel Sigismondo.

It was not really surprising that the Renaissance princes built churches and palaces, and commissioned artists to make works of art. Since the earliest days of Christian Europe, men to whom God had given good fortune

Sigismondo Malatesta, who was called the worst scoundrel in Italy, had himself painted at prayer.

This bust of a smiling, gap-toothed woman was done in majolica, a kind of pottery.

had shown their gratitude by beautifying churches and monasteries. Building for God and adorning God's buildings were a part of the Christian life. After all, it was the most dramatic way of reaching and teaching those who could not read. Therefore it was only natural that as men became wealthy in Venice, in Florence, in Milan, they spent some of their wealth on their parish churches, on monasteries and nunneries, and on the cathedrals in their cities.

In doing this, they followed the example of the Pope himself. At Avignon, and later at Rome, the works of art made for the popes were the envy of the kings of Europe as well as the princes of Italy. To all men, even the most strict in their religion, pictures of sacred objects were a part of religion as old as the Church itself.

It had also long been the custom of rulers to adorn their palaces. They liked metalwork and jewelry; they liked to read their prayers from costly books. Most of all, perhaps, they liked tapestries and frescoes—wall paintings—that told a favorite story, or reminded them of things they enjoyed doing, such as hunting. By 1400, however, there were hundreds of merchants in Italy who could afford the beautiful objects that once could be owned only by aristocrats. These merchants came from the cities. Often their families had become great as the city had become great. They were proud of their wealth and position, and wished to show this in the buildings, statues, and decorations of their cities. The city-states of Renaissance Italy competed for works of art as well as for power. It added to the greatness of a king to have famous artists attached to his court. The city-states, especially Florence and Venice, were as proud of their artists as any king.

Money and energy were poured into the arts, opening up careers to men who might have turned to other kinds of work. Any poor peasant boy who showed some ability was likely to find a sponsor among the neighboring noblemen or local merchants. Of course, many of the artists came from the families of craftsmen—the jewelers, goldsmiths, metalworkers, and decorative painters—in which they could become apprentices at an early age. Yet, like the Church, the arts attracted men of many different backgrounds, and this in itself had a good effect.

Besides competition for artists, there was

Only a knowledge of science kept artists from being classified with mere craftsmen, such as the sculptor who is shown here with masons and bricklayers.

competition between artists. In the Middle Ages, a craftsman could spend a lifetime beautifying one cathedral or monastery. He cared nothing about his reputation with the public or rivalry with fellow artists. By 1450, personal feuds and rivalry between artists had become common in Venice and Florence. This again was good for art, because each artist tried to develop his own style. Not that every painting was done by only one man. A successful painter of the Renaissance was the head of a workshop with many apprentices. Often it was a family affair in which brothers, sons, and even daughters joined. Painters also used helpers who specialized in hands or costumes or backgrounds.

Still, everything about the Renaissance encouraged the artist to develop his own way of painting, different from that of other artists. And the rewards were so large that artists took risks which craftsmen in earlier days would never have dared to take. They devoted themselves completely to art; nothing else mattered. Andrea del Castagno was said to have killed another artist, Domenico, out of envy. Piero di Cosimo boiled the eggs he lived on,

fifty at once, with his varnishes to save time.

Stories such as these may or may not have been true, but they showed how Renaissance Italy expected its artists to live. The crowd of painters, sculptors, goldsmiths, decorators, and jewelers contained men of many different abilities and personalities—men like Leonardo da Vinci, who was deeply curious; like Michelangelo, who had a powerful imagination; like Piero della Francesca, who had great intellect; like Raphael, who was a brilliant craftsman.

To improve their art, artists studied works from the past, studied nature, studied the sciences. They were particularly fascinated by perspective, the method of showing objects as they appear at various distances from the viewer. Brunelleschi demonstrated the new theories of perspective with the aid of mathematics. Soon artists were studying optics, writing textbooks on geometry, and using mathematics to work out details of their compositions. They drew hats, mountains, and even people in the shape of geometric forms. They painted tile pavements and rows of columns that seemed to go off into the

In Madonna and Child, *the artist Piero della Francesca used an egg and a shell as religious symbols.*

distance. Uccello painted many pictures to demonstrate his skill in handling difficult problems of perspective. The greatest mathematician among the artists was Piero della Francesca, who finally gave up art for mathematics and painted nothing for the last fourteen years of his life.

Artists studied anatomy and filled their notebooks with measured drawings of the human figure. Anatomy lessons became part of an artist's training. Artists followed the advice of the scholar Alberti, who said in a

book on painting, "Begin with the bones, then add the muscles, and then cover the body with flesh in such a way as to leave the position of the muscles visible." It was said that Signorelli was so interested in the scientific study of the human body that he dissected the corpse of his own son. In time, however, the artists stopped displaying their knowledge of anatomy. Instead, they tried to bring out the beauty of the nude figures of men and women.

The painting of the nude, as well as that of landscape and portraits, developed slowly. In early Renaissance art, landscape was used as a symbol. Terrible mountains, rocks, and forests, for example, stood for hell and horror. Then a Flemish artist, Jan van Eyck, began giving small background landscapes to his altarpieces—pictures painted for the altars of churches. Both his feeling for landscape and his knowledge of oil paints were taken back to Italy. Artists began to experiment with color, light, and shade.

As the princes cleared the highways of robbers and set up model farms, people began to be interested in the Italian countryside. Poets wrote about the joys of country living. Painters followed their lead, placing saints and the Holy Family in a landscape of gentle meadows and hills. They used local landscape as background in scenes from the Bible, and showed views of the countryside beyond the shoulder of persons in portraits. During the Middle Ages, men had felt that nature was hostile. During the Renaissance, men felt completely at home in nature, and finally the landscape itself became the most important thing in a painting.

Portraits were first painted to glorify the great, but as time went on, even merchants could commission artists to do their pictures. One Renaissance scholar said that the laws of antiquity had forbidden artists to paint the portrait of anyone who was not a prince or a wise and virtuous man. Now, he complained, anyone could have his picture painted. Artists continued to glorify princes, but they also tried to show the true character of people. "Paint the face," Leonardo da Vinci said, "in such a way that it will be easy to understand what is going on in the mind."

By the time the Renaissance reached its height, art was an accepted part of life. Artists were consulted on all kinds of things, from the arrangement of a table to the construction of fortifications. Most of the great artists were Jacks-of-all-trades. They were astoundingly versatile. Michelangelo was chiefly a sculptor, but he also painted frescoes, designed buildings, and, when he was in the right mood, wrote poetry. Leonardo da Vinci was not too proud to design costumes for a masquerade or fix the heating for a duchess' bath. Applying for a job in 1482, the thirty-year-old Leonardo wrote to Lodovico of Milan:

Most Illustrious Lord, having now sufficiently seen and considered the proofs of all those who count themselves masters and inventors of instruments of war, and finding that their invention and use of the said instruments does not differ in any respect from those in common practice, I am emboldened without prejudice to anyone else to put myself in communication with your Excellency, in order to acquaint you with my secrets, thereafter offering myself at your pleasure effectually to demonstrate at any convenient time all those matters which are in part briefly recorded below.
1. I have plans for bridges, very light and strong and suitable for carrying very easily....
2. When a place is besieged I know how to cut off water from the trenches, and how to construct an infinite number of . . . scaling ladders and other instruments. . . .

Giorgione used landscape to soften the composition of his painting, the Castelfranco Madonna.

3. Also if a place cannot be reduced by the method of bombardment, either through the height of its glacis or the strength of its position, I have plans for destroying every fortress or other stronghold unless it has been founded upon rock.
4. I have plans for making cannon, very convenient and easy of transport, with which to hurl small stones in the manner almost of hail. . . .
5. And if it should happen that the engagement is at sea, I have plans for constructing

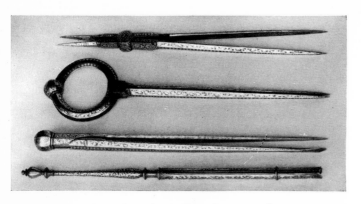

Draftsmen's tools, made in the sixteenth century.

many engines most suitable for attack or defense, and ships which can resist the fire of all the heaviest cannon....

6. Also I have ways of arriving at a fixed spot by caverns and secret winding passages, made without any noise even though it may be necessary to pass underneath trenches or a river.

7. Also I can make armored cars, safe and unassailable, which will enter the serried ranks of the enemy with artillery, and there is no company of men at arms so great as not to be broken by it. And behind these the infantry will be able to follow quite unharmed and without opposition.

8. Also, if need shall arise, I can make cannon, mortars, and light ordnance of very beautiful and useful shapes, quite different from those in common use.

9. Where it is not possible to employ cannon, I can supply catapults, mangonels, traps, and other engines of wonderful efficacy not in general use. In short, as the variety of circumstances shall necessitate, I can supply an infinite number of different engines of attack and defense.

10. In time of peace I believe that I can give you as complete satisfaction as anyone else in architecture, in the construction of buildings both public and private, and in conducting water from one place to another.

Also I can execute sculpture in marble, bronze, or clay, and also painting, in which my work will stand comparison with that of anyone else whoever he may be.

Moreover, I would undertake the work of the bronze horse, which shall endue with immortal glory and eternal honor the auspicious memory of the Prince your father and of the illustrious house of Sforza.

And if any of the aforesaid things should seem impossible or impracticable to anyone, I

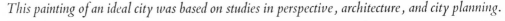

This painting of an ideal city was based on studies in perspective, architecture, and city planning.

offer myself as ready to make trial of them in your park or in whatever place shall please your Excellency, to whom I commend myself with all possible humility.

The versatility of Leonardo and Michelangelo was far from unusual. Princes and wealthy merchants wished to be surrounded by art. They wanted pageantry, masquerades, feasts, dancing, and music. They delighted in pleasing their senses and in impressing other people, and they were willing to pay for it. They would call on the great masters of painting for even the smallest kind of job— the molding of pastry, the decoration of a table, the casting of a candlestick, the design of a dagger.

And so art was part of everyday living, part of the life of man. The scholars, too, were concerned with the life of man on this earth, with human beings. In fact, they called themselves humanists, and their studies they called the humanities. Like Ciriaco de' Pizzicolli, they awakened the dead. They searched for knowledge in the writings of the ancient past, reading again and again the classics of Greece and Rome.

They gave much thought to the problems of princes and cities. They asked: What made men succeed—or fail? Why did some cities grow great and rich, only to lose it all in war and rebellion? Why did free citizens become the victims of professional thugs? What were the causes of tyranny? Was tyranny bad? Did cities have a natural life, like men? Did philosophers make the best citizens?

The humanists were interested in the lives and actions of men, not in the mysteries of God. As advisers and secretaries to princes and popes, they helped to change the thinking of rulers. But the Church still remained a power, and religion continued to be a force during the Renaissance.

Princes and their followers; popes and their cardinals, bishops, priests, and monks; condottieri and their soldiers; merchants and their guilds; artists and their apprentices; craftsmen and their helpers; humanists and their students—all made up the brilliant pageant of the Renaissance. And then there were the masses of people, who worked the land, who obeyed the princes and sometimes rebelled against them, who prayed in the splendid churches, who suffered war and famine and plague, and yet somehow managed to live and love, to eat and sleep and labor and rear children.

The Renaissance was an exciting age, an adventurous age, an age of discovery and rediscovery, of exploration and examination. It was also an age of tyranny and treachery, of brutality and crime. It meant the end of the Middle Ages and the beginning of modern times, for in that age the spirit of man seemed to flame and burn with a magnificent light that brightened every corner of the Western world. And nowhere in Italy did the flame burn brighter than it did in the four great city-states of Florence, Milan, Rome, and Venice.

A RENAISSANCE IN ART

Even before the Renaissance, there were some artists who broke away from the stiff, formal style of the art of the Middle Ages. Among them was Giotto, who, with the sculptor Andrea Pisano, did the bas-reliefs (right) for the campanile, or bell tower, at Florence. It was works like these, realistic and full of life, that led to such Renaissance masterpieces as the frescoes (some of which are shown at left) in the church of San Francesco in Arezzo. They tell the story of the True Cross. The artist, Piero della Francesca, began painting them in 1452 but did not complete them until twelve years later.

29

Weeping angels hover in the air in the Pietà *(below), one of the scenes from the life of Christ painted by Giotto. Giotto influenced many Renaissance painters, and in his own day was famous through-out Italy. Once, when an agent of the Papacy asked for a sample of his work, Giotto drew a perfect circle with one stroke of his brush and told the agent to send it back to Rome. The realism of the artists who followed Giotto is shown in* Saint Jerome in His Study *(opposite, top) by Antonello da Messina, who learned both the technique of oil painting and the use of great detail from the Flemish. Realism of a less detailed kind is shown in a section of a painting by Fra Angelico (opposite, below), depicting workmen unloading wheat.*

Renaissance painters were fascinated by the scientific study of art,
and experimented with perspective and the use of geometric forms.
Sometimes they worked out their compositions mathematically, as
Piero della Francesca did in the Flagellation of Christ (below).

Artists filled their sketchbooks with carefully measured drawings of the human figure, like the full face (right) by Leonardo da Vinci and the tilted face (far right) by Piero della Francesca.

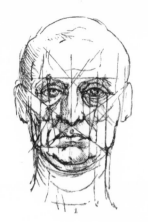
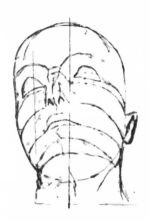

Paolo Uccello, who was a master of perspective, liked to draw detailed studies of complex forms, such as a swirling rosette of ribbons (above) or a goblet (below).

*Renaissance portraits often reveal the character of their subjects, as in
Leonardo da Vinci's painting of Cecilia Gallerani (below) and Sandro
Botticelli's painting of Giovanni di Pierfrancesco de' Medici (opposite).*

*Portrait medals, in imitation of ancient coins, were
commissioned by princes, humanists, and merchants,
who sent them to friends as mementos. Leonello
d'Este is shown on this medal by Antonio Pisanello.*

Anatomy lessons were part of the training of Renaissance artists, and they made innumerable studies of the nude human figure, like Luca Signorelli's drawing of a muscular man (below). Italian artists had been studying anatomy for more than a century when Titian painted Diana and Actaeon (left), a scene from Greek mythology.

In this detail from The Adoration of the Shepherds
*(above) by Giorgione, the landscape is calm and serene.
Lazzaro Bastiani placed St. Jerome in a frankly fantastic
landscape (below), beside a rocky highway to heaven.*

Deeply interested in nature, Renaissance artists made landscape an important part of their pictures. Giovanni Bellini's Saint Francis in Ecstasy *shows how carefully the artist studied the Italian countryside.*

FLORENCE, CRADLE OF THE RENAISSANCE

The city of Florence was the cradle of the Renaissance—and yet in its cathedral preached Savonarola, the monk who would have nothing to do with the Renaissance. It was a city known for its painters, sculptors, scholars, and philosophers—and yet it was a city of merchants. It was a city that loved freedom and liberty—and yet it fell under the rule of tyrants. The city knew little freedom under Lorenzo the Magnificent—and yet it was said that no tyrant could be better or more pleasing.

Florence was a city of contrasts even in its geography. Its landscape was gentle, yet its location made the facts of its life not gentle, but brutal. To the west, controlling its only outlet to the sea, lay prosperous and powerful Pisa. Across the route to Pisa was Lucca, an unbeatable enemy. To the north was Milan, hungry for land and rich in men and money. To the south, Siena controlled the road to Rome, as proud and warlike as Florence itself. And to the east were the small tyrants who lived like wolves, by war and violence and plunder.

To exist at all, let alone expand, Florence needed citizens who were courageous and clever. They had to practice diplomacy as well as war, and both took money. And it was wealth, after all, that allowed Florence to survive and grow and become great, in spite of its location.

A view of Florence, with the great dome of the cathedral gleaming in the sunlight, between the campanile and the tower of the Palazzo Vecchio.

The emblem of the wool merchants' guild

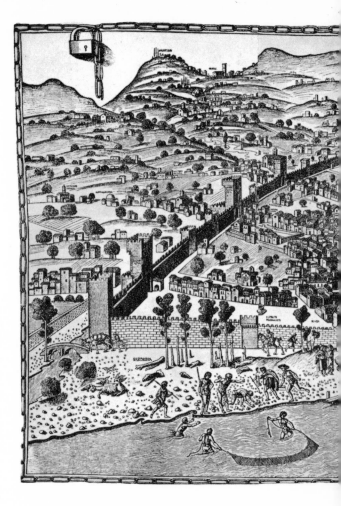

A woodcut of Florence, made about 1486.

Florence's wealth and strength came from its merchants. In 1472 Benedetto Dei could write, "Our beautiful Florence contains within the city in this present year two hundred seventy shops belonging to the wool merchants' guild, from whence their wares are sent to Rome and the Marches, Naples and Sicily, Constantinople and Pera, Adrianople, Broussa, and the whole of Turkey. It contains also eighty-three rich and splendid warehouses of the silk merchants' guild, and furnishes gold and silver stuffs, velvet, brocade, damask, taffeta, and satin to Rome, Naples, Catalonia, and the whole of Spain, especially Seville, and to Turkey and Barbary. . . . The number of banks amounts to thirty-three; the shops of the cabinet-makers, whose business is carving and inlaid work, to eighty-four; and the workshops of the stone-cutters and marble workers in the city and its immediate neighborhood, to fifty-four. There are forty-four goldsmiths' and jewellers' shops, thirty gold-beaters, silver-wire drawers, and a wax-figure maker. . . . Another flourishing industry is the making of light and elegant gold and silver wreaths and garlands, which are worn by young maidens of high degree. . . . Sixty-six is the number of the apothecaries' and grocer shops; seventy that of the butchers, besides eight large shops in which are sold fowls of all kinds, as well as game and also the native wine. . . ."

If Florence's strength came from its merchants, the merchants' strength came from their guilds. Strongest of all, and one of the earliest, was the guild known as the *arte di Calimala*. This was a company of merchants who traded with England, France, and Flanders. They brought in cloth to Florence, where it was reworked and dyed in bright, splendid colors—blues and crimsons and reds. The finished goods were exported throughout Europe, and the stamp of the guild became a guarantee of value and workmanship. The guild was well ruled, and it regulated its members' moral life as well as their public life.

In the center of the walled section on the right of the Arno River is the Pitti palace.

Altogether, including the *Calimala*, there were seven principal guilds—the wool merchants, the silk weavers, the bankers, the notaries, the druggists (who also dealt in spices and precious stones), and the furriers. The seven included all the great merchants of Florence, who formed the heart of its business and financial life. But Florence was a large town, in the midst of a well-populated countryside, and its shopkeepers were numerous enough to form their own guilds. There were fourteen of these lesser guilds—the innkeepers, shoemakers, carpenters, blacksmiths, grocers, bakers, and the like.

The officers of each guild included one who carried its special banner in the great processions that took place on the day of its patron saint. Each guild had a church which its members attended, and in which were held its special masses. The Florentine guilds were closely regulated. They carefully guarded their rights and customs, and they had much power.

There was often bad feeling between the greater guilds and the lesser guilds. The lesser guilds felt that their numbers gave them a right to power. The greater guilds felt that it was their money that supported the government of Florence, in both peace and war. Yet there never were more than three or four thousand men in all the twenty-one guilds, and Florence had a population of nearly a hundred thousand. Most of the people worked for a day's wages, spinning, dyeing, weaving,

The angel over the grain market calls for rejoicing at abundance, but warns that scarcity may follow.

carding, or hauling the huge bales of wool and cloth and silk. They were the citizens who, in the very beginning, fought for the liberties within the city and for its rich territories outside the city.

They were organized into four districts, each with four quarters. From the quarters were chosen the governors of the city who made up the Signory. The Signory ruled Florence, made war or peace, and decided on taxes. But its chief officers, the priors, ruled for only two months, and then gave way to another group.

To control the government, men fought in the streets, murdered, and destroyed each other. So many Florentines were exiled that one citizen remarked there were enough men in exile to populate another city. The question was whether government should be in the hands of a few men or many, whether the greater guilds or the lesser guilds should have more power, and Florentines fought over who should be the priors. Sometimes, too, the people rebelled and snatched power out of the hands of the mighty—but never for long.

In 1402, Florence was about to be taken by Gian Galeazzo Visconti of Milan. Suddenly, in the prime of life and with success just ahead, Gian Galeazzo sickened and died. The Florentines were sure this had not happened by chance. They believed that they carried on the traditions of ancient Rome, and that they were republicans who had defeated a tyrant. After the lucky death of Galeazzo, they won one battle after another. At the same time, their trade rose and wealth poured into the city. Florence was still free, still republican, and never had it been so prosperous and famous. Its artists and scholars went about their tasks with new energy, and humanism was encouraged.

Then, in 1417, the most powerful member of the ruling group died, and once again there was a struggle for control of the government. And when the struggle was over, Florence found that the Medici family was the most powerful in the city. Head of the family was Giovanni di Bicci de' Medici. He had built up the Medici's banking business until it had branches in sixteen European capitals. A quiet, modest man, he stayed away from politics. He spent his money on charity, art, and the construction of churches. He was considered a good, safe man, and no threat to anyone. But in 1421 he was chosen gonfalonier, head of the Signory. He supported a new kind of tax; each person would pay according to his wealth and income. Up to this time the rich had paid no more than the poor, and now they set up a great howl.

Giovanni died in 1429, mourned by the people. His son, Cosimo, who became the head of the family, followed in his footsteps. He was as modest and charitable as his father. Cosimo, too, minded his own business carefully, and that business was constantly growing. The rich had not forgotten about the tax, and they waited their chance to hit back at the Medici. They were led by the Albizzi, a rival family which was plotting with the nobles. In 1433 they succeeded in getting their own men

Cosimo de' Medici, banker and patron of the arts

in the Signory, and they decided to act. They charged that the Medici were a danger to the state because of their wealth and ambition. Among other things, Cosimo was accused of building a new mansion whose size and style were not fitting for a private citizen.

Cosimo was arrested and thrown into prison, and the Albizzi called for the death sentence. But, with the help of a jailer, Cosimo smuggled out a big bribe to the head of the Signory. Instead of death, Cosimo and all his family were sentenced to exile for ten years. He moved to Venice, where he made many friends. A year went by, and a new Signory was elected, a Signory friendly to the Medici. It canceled the sentence of exile, and Cosimo returned to Florence and was given a warm welcome.

Now it was the Albizzi's turn to leave the city. They fled, and two hundred of their followers were exiled or killed. When Cosimo heard complaints that he was being too hard on the aristocrats, he remarked that new ones could be made with two lengths of crimson cloth. States could not be ruled by prayers. "Better a city destroyed than lost," he added.

Cosimo saw to it that he did not lose the city. While he himself held office in the government for only a few years, he ruled through his friends—and through his money. As banker to the republic, he was in a strong position. He adjusted taxes in favor of his friends and against his enemies. Once in a while he used violence. Baldaccio d'Anghiari, who was suspected of plotting against him, was thrown out of a high window, and Cosimo did not object.

Yet he served the city wisely and well. He made generous loans to the republic, and he paid many expenses, such as entertaining distinguished visitors, out of his own pocket. Like his father, he loved peace and avoided war. In the past, Florence had always allied

45

itself with Venice against Milan. But when Venice threatened to take Milan and win rule of most of northern Italy, Cosimo changed the policy. He supported Francesco Sforza, who stopped the Venetian advance. When Venice and Naples turned against Cosimo, he called in so many loans from citizens of the two cities that they stopped their military operations. After that, Florence and Milan were allies. Both sides were about equally strong; neither dared to make war. This gave Italy years of peace in which her cities became wealthy.

With all his riches and power, Cosimo lived simply. He was up early every day, tending to his many business and political affairs. He did not wear gorgeous clothes. He entertained visitors with elaborate feasts, but only the plainest of food was served at the meals he took alone with his family.

Again like his father, he spent large sums of money on churches and art. He employed such architects as Brunelleschi and Michelozzo, such sculptors as Donatello and Luca della Robbia, such painters as Fra Angelico, Filippo Lippi, and Benozzo Gozzoli. He loved learning, and was himself extremely well educated. He knew Latin, and a little Greek, Hebrew, and Arabic. He sent agents abroad to search for rare books for his library, and paid forty-five men to copy manuscripts he could not buy.

In his old age, crippled by gout, Cosimo worried about the future of his family. One of his two sons died; the other was sickly. As the old man was carried through the rooms of his mansion, he murmured, "Too large a house for so small a family." He was seventy-five when he died in 1464, and on his tomb were inscribed the Latin words *Pater Patriae*—the Father of his Country.

In the last years of his life, the old and weary Cosimo had lost control of his followers. They outraged Florence by their dishonesty and the way they trampled on the rights of others. Cosimo left behind him confusion and disorder. He also left an invalid son, Piero, who had gout, a mild disposition, and treacherous advisers.

Piero lived and ruled for only five years after the death of Cosimo. But during those years he did one thing which set the reputation of his son, Lorenzo. He arranged a marriage between the nineteen-year-old boy and a member of the Orsini family, which was among the most aristocratic families in Rome. The Florentines grumbled, remembering that Cosimo had made it a rule to marry the Medici at home. Now the Medici were getting too ambitious; soon they would be acting like aristocrats themselves.

The betrothal was celebrated by a tournament, something unfamiliar in Florence. It was described as ". . . a scuffle of men on horseback in which the leading young men of the city contended with the most renowned cavaliers of Italy; and among the Florentine youth the most famous was Lorenzo, who carried off the prize not by favor but by his own valor." Clothed in gorgeous armor, the muscular young athlete easily unhorsed all his opponents. The Florentines were so proud of him that they decided the marriage wasn't so bad, after all. Piero gave Lorenzo a magnificent wedding feast—and magnificent became the word for Lorenzo. In time, he would actually be called Lorenzo the Magnificent. But long before that, Lorenzo learned how valuable magnificence was in politics, and he developed a taste for it.

When Piero died, Lorenzo became head of the Medici family. "Two days after the death of my father," he later wrote, "although I,

Ladies, red-robed merchants, and boys squinting through peepholes watch a tournament in Florence.

Lorenzo, was very young, being only in my twenty-first year, the principal men of the city came to our house to condole on our loss and encourage me to take on myself the care of the city and the state, as my father and grandfather had done. This proposal being contrary to the instincts of my youthful age and considering that the burden and danger were great, I consented unwillingly, but I did so to protect our friends and property, for it fares ill in Florence with anyone who possesses great wealth without any control in the government."

More fortunate than his father, Lorenzo found faithful and loyal friends. With the aid of a group of prominent citizens who wanted to stop disorder in Florence, he began governing under unusually good conditions. The first nine years were peaceful and fairly easy, and Lorenzo seemed to be the most fortunate of his family.

Unlike his father and his grandfather, he was a young man when he became head of the Medici. Like most young men, he wanted to enjoy the pleasures of life. He made Florence a city of festivals, with masquerades and revels, pageants and processions. He hired the best artists to design the masks and decorate the

The armored knights could be easily identified by the names embroidered on their bridles.

floats. He took part in the festivities himself, and wrote songs and poems for them. In this, too, he was different from his ancestors. They had taken many risks, but they had never dared to write verses.

Not everyone approved of Lorenzo. A Florentine historian wrote that Lorenzo "desired glory and excellence above all other men and can be criticized for having had too much ambition even in minor things; he did not want to be equalled or imitated even in verses or games or exercises and turned angrily on anyone who did so."

Still, for nine years all went well. They were years of peace and plenty, and wisely Lorenzo made the most of them. As he himself wrote:

> How passing fair is youth,
> Forever fleeting away;
> Who happy would be, let him be;
> Of tomorrow who can say?

"Of tomorrow who can say?" There was truth in these words, for already, as he was writing them, the uncertain tomorrow was approaching. In 1478 came the most fearful of all the plots against the Medici—the Pazzi conspiracy.

The Pazzi were an old, proud, and wealthy family, with more reasons to consider them-

A Florentine shield painted with the figure of David

selves aristocrats than the Medici. They had never been given the positions in the government or the honors to which they were entitled, and they were bitter. The most bitter of the Pazzi was Francesco. Unable to stand it any longer, he went off to Rome, where he happened to fall in with one of the six nephews of the ambitious Pope Sixtus IV. The two hatched a plot against the Medici, which the Pope agreed to support. Francesco hurried back to Florence to tell his family the news. Jacopo de' Pazzi, the head of the family, hesitated only until he was sure that the scheme had the blessing of the Pope.

It was the Pope who began the campaign against the Medici. He took away the privileges of the Medici bank in Rome and gave them to the Pazzi. Then he appointed as

Archbishop of Pisa a member of the Salviati family, who were also enemies of the Medici.

Lorenzo seems to have suspected nothing. In April, 1478, the conspirators gathered in Florence, where they were entertained by Lorenzo. They planned to kill Lorenzo and his brother Giuliano during a banquet. But Giuliano failed to attend the banquet, and both brothers had to be killed if the scheme was to succeed. The murders were postponed until the following morning, during High Mass in the Duomo, the cathedral. It would be the morning of Easter Sunday, and the conspirators were sure both brothers would appear in church.

The change in plan almost upset the plot. The man hired to take charge of the killings refused to commit murder in the cathedral. Two priests then offered to attack Lorenzo; Francesco de' Pazzi and Bernardo Bandini would kill Giuliano. But there was still another hitch. On Sunday morning, Giuliano was not at the Duomo. He was at home, in bed with a bad knee. Francesco and Bernardo hurried to his house. Smiling and joking, they coaxed him out of bed. They held him up between them, embracing him fondly—not forgetting to feel his body to make sure he was unarmed —and brought him, limping, to the church.

Lorenzo, also unarmed, had by this time taken his place in the crowded cathedral. All was ready for the murders. The signal was to be the moment in the Mass when the priest raised the Host and the worshipers bowed their heads. That moment came; the priest raised the Host; hundreds of heads bowed.

Giuliano, too, obediently bowed his head. Bernardo, standing behind him, struck the first blow, and Giuliano fell. Francesco finished him off, stabbing him with a dagger eighteen times. So furiously did he stab that he hacked himself in the leg. The two other conspirators leaped at Lorenzo with their daggers. Defending himself as best he could, Lorenzo escaped with a gash in the neck. His friends quickly surrounded him and they ran into the sacristy, where they bolted the doors and waited for help.

Meanwhile, Archbishop Salviati and a band of followers were entering the palace to seize the government. While he went to an upper floor to talk to the Signory, most of his companions waited below, where by mistake they locked themselves into a room. The members of the Signory saw that the Archbishop was nervous and excited. They became suspicious, guessed why he had come, and hanged him from the window.

The city was now in an uproar. Francesco de' Pazzi, bleeding from the wound he had given himself, had been taken home. From his bed he begged his uncle, Jacopo de' Pazzi, to rally the people to their cause. Jacopo led a hundred armed men through the streets, shouting "Liberty! Liberty!" But the people answered with shouts for the Medici, and Jacopo fled. Lorenzo, escorted by his friends, returned home unharmed.

Francesco was dragged from his bed by a mob and hanged from the palace window beside the Archbishop. Anyone even suspected of having anything to do with the plot was hunted down. Seventy men were killed in four days; two hundred more before the man-hunt was over. Jacopo de' Pazzi: caught and killed, was not allowed to rest in his grave. His body was unearthed, dragged through the streets, and thrown naked into the river. Of his ten sons and nephews, two were beheaded. One of the sons was saved by Lorenzo, who was his brother-in-law. The rest were sentenced to imprisonment or exile.

The Pope was in a rage over the failure of the plot. He demanded that Lorenzo surrender and that the Signory be tried by a Church court for killing the Archbishop. Lorenzo pro-tested that his only crime was that he had not allowed himself to be murdered, and the Signory stood by him. It made public a confession by one of the conspirators which told of the Pope's part in the plot, and asked the rulers of Europe for support. They sided with the Medici. The Pope excommunicated the Florentine state; the Florentine priests in turn outlawed him; and the Pope declared war. He forbade any Catholic from trading with the Florentines. He broke all their alliances with other states, and prohibited new ones. No soldier was allowed to fight for them. Calling to his aid Siena and Naples, he sent their troops into Tuscany.

The fighting went badly for the Florentines, and Lorenzo offered to surrender himself. The

Giuliano de' Medici was murdered in the cathedral.

Pico della Mirandola, one of the leading humanists attracted to Lorenzo's court, was said to be the master of twenty-two languages. Among his teachers and friends were several Jews, and he was a student of the Cabala, a strange, mystic Hebrew philosophy feared even by the rabbis. It was Pico who wrote that man "can be that which he wills to be . . . ."

Signory refused to hear of it. But he slipped off to Naples, where he negotiated with King Ferrante. Although Ferrante was known to be treacherous, he was impressed by Lorenzo's daring. He treated Lorenzo like a guest rather than a prisoner, listened to his arguments, and agreed to stop helping the Pope. The Pope was furious, but he had other and more serious troubles. The Turks were moving westward, and their troops threatened to overrun all Italy. The Pope, too, decided to make peace with Lorenzo and the Florentines.

After the Pazzi conspiracy, Lorenzo was determined not to let anything like it happen again. He surrounded himself with an armed guard and tightened his control of the government. He set up a council, responsible to himself alone, that had more power than the Signory. Instead of ruling through friends and money, he became a dictator. At the same time, he became a much more skillful statesman, and he worked hard to keep the peace in Italy.

Now that Florence was safe again, some of its citizens began to criticize Lorenzo. They said his trip to Naples had been foolish and unnecessary. He might have accomplished just as much by staying home, instead of risking his life and returning as a hero. By handling the Pope more gently, he might have prevented the war, which had harmed trade and sent taxes higher. And his punishment of the Pazzi was too cruel. He should not have imprisoned the innocent young men of the family and forbade the Pazzi girls to marry.

Later, however, as the historian Guicciardini wrote, "softened by time, he gave permission for the maidens to marry and was willing to release the Pazzi from prison and let them go and live outside of Florentine territory. And also it was seen that he did not employ cruelty in other matters and was not a bloodthirsty person." But for a long while Lorenzo kept a careful watch on the city's most important families. He would allow none of their members to marry without his consent, and often arranged marriages himself.

Nevertheless, there was peace in Florence, and again Lorenzo turned to the things he loved most in life—women and art and learning. The Medici had always spent money on art. Cosimo had poured out wealth on buildings—palaces, monasteries, churches—on sculpture and on paintings. In the Medici palaces were pictures and statues, antique busts and painted shields, goblets, tapestries, a unicorn's horn set in gold, a collection of more than five thousand ancient coins and cameos. Under Lorenzo, the family kept a sculptor, Bertoldo, who looked after the collections of ancient art and taught apprentices in the garden.

Lorenzo made Florence the capital of art and learning in Italy. He set the pace, and other princes were forced to compete. He bid the highest for the services of artists and scholars, and carried off the best of them. In Pisa he set up a branch of the University of Florence, just for the pleasure of outdoing other schools. He went to great expense and trouble to bring in the most famous teachers in Italy. Philosophers were part of his household; debates and discussions were carried on even at his dinner table. Scholars held such a high place in Florence that one of them boasted, "The whole state is turned to look at me." And, indeed, crowds flocked to the scholars' public lectures.

Learning brought Lorenzo relief from the cares of governing the state. Educated as a boy by humanists, he was one of them. He spent more than half the annual income of the state on books, and enormous sums on art. Artists gathered in Florence from near and far, and not only for the money Lorenzo paid. He appreciated their abilities, understood their problems, and defended them against fools. Poets gathered in Florence, too, and musicians and architects, and Lorenzo helped them all.

As Lorenzo grew older, he grew more mellow. Guicciardini wrote, "Though the city was not free under him, it would have been impossible to find a better or more pleasing tyrant. From his natural goodness and inclination came infinite advantages, but through the necessity of tyranny some evils although they were restrained and limited as much as necessity permitted. . . ."

For twelve years following the Pazzi conspiracy, Florence enjoyed its Golden Age. Then Lorenzo became ill with gout, and, even worse, had trouble in his business dealings. He dipped into money that belonged to the city, so that Florence almost went bankrupt. He saved his private fortune by investing in land, but it cost him his good name.

The merchants of the city, especially those that dealt in cloth, were in trouble, too. The English were beginning to make their own cloth; the Flemish were reworking and dyeing cloth as skillfully as the Italians. Trade with the East was falling. The poor became even poorer. Many of them died of the fevers and consumption that raged like a fire in the filthy slums. Suffering in the midst of riches, the people turned to religion—and they listened to the thundering voice of Savonarola.

Savonarola was a Dominican monk at the monastery of San Marco. It had been founded by Cosimo Medici and had received much money from Lorenzo. That made no difference to Savonarola. He preached against dishonest priests, he preached against the bankers, and he preached against Lorenzo. More and more people came to hear his sermons, in one of which he said:

"The people are oppressed by taxes, and when they come to pay unbearable sums, the rich cry: Give me the rest. . . . When widows come weeping, they are told: Go to sleep. When the poor complain, they are told: Pay, pay."

Lorenzo sent gifts to San Marco. Savonarola said that a dog does not stop barking in defense of his master because it has been thrown a bone. San Marco was too small to hold the crowds that came to hear him, and he moved to the Duomo. The huge cathedral was packed to the doors when he stepped into the pulpit. He predicted that God would send a calamity which would sweep away the princes of Italy, including the Medici.

Lorenzo was troubled. Savonarola might do with his fiery words what the Pazzi could not do with their flashing daggers. Lorenzo sent a delegation to talk to the monk. His sermons were disturbing the city and might lead to violence; Lorenzo might decide to banish him.

Savonarola replied, "Tell Lorenzo to do penance for his sins, for God will punish him and his. I do not fear your banishments. Though I am a stranger here and he a citizen, and the foremost in the city, I shall remain and he will go. I shall remain," he repeated proudly, "and he will go." And he foretold the death of Lorenzo within a year.

Lorenzo did not try to interfere with Savonarola again. A year later, Lorenzo lay dying, in great pain from a stomach disorder. His doctors fed him powdered pearls, which only made him worse. As he tossed on his bed, lightning struck the great dome of the cathedral.

"Behold," shouted Savonarola, "the sword of the Lord, swift and sure over the peoples of the earth!"

Lorenzo sent for Savonarola to relieve his soul, and the monk came to his side. Later a story was told about their meeting. It was said that the monk made three demands. He asked Lorenzo to repent his sins, rid himself of his wealth, and give up the power of the Medici so that Florence would once again have its liberty. Lorenzo agreed to the first two. But he could not bring himself to agree to the third, and died before his sins were forgiven. At least, so went the story.

That was in 1492, and Lorenzo's eldest son, Piero, became head of the Medici. A poor ruler, he became known as Piero the Unfortunate. Savonarola's power grew even greater. He warned that the sins of Italy's tyrants and priests would bring on a terrible disaster. A Florentine said his sermons "caused such terror, alarm, sobbing, and tears that everyone passed through the streets without speaking, more dead than alive."

In the early months of 1494, Savonarola predicted that King Charles VIII of France would invade Italy. By September his prediction had come true. By November, Charles was in Florentine territory. But the French were not really interested in Florence; it was Naples they wanted. They left Florence to the Florentines, but only after Piero agreed to surrender certain territories to the French for as long as the war lasted. He also agreed that the city would give Charles a huge sum of money. He had done all this without consulting the Signory, which decided that it wanted no more of his rule. Jeered and stoned in the streets, Piero and the rest of the Medici family fled to Venice. A mob broke into their palace and stole or destroyed the precious works of art the Medici had been collecting for years.

Florence again became a republic, but Savonarola was the real power in the land. Acting on his advice, the government passed laws against gambling, swearing, immoral songs, and horse racing. Groups of boys from Savonarola's congregation, called "bands of hope," went out into the streets. They collected money for the church, broke up gambling games, and tore fancy dresses from the backs of women. For a while Florence was a changed city. People dressed in plain clothes, gave money to charity, and crowded the churches. Savonarola said that the real ruler of the city should be Christ Himself, and that it could set an example for Italy and the rest of the world.

But the Medici still had friends in Florence, and there were many others who hated the power of Savonarola, or the changes he had brought about. They called his followers *Piagnoni*, or snivelers, because of the weeping that went on during the monk's sermons. The *Piagnoni*, in turn, called their enemies *Arrabbiati*, or mad dogs. Snivelers or mad dogs, the Florentines were going through a bad time. They were losing territory; they were losing trade. Months of heavy rain spoiled the crops, and people were falling dead of starvation. Many Florentines turned against Savonarola, and *Piagnoni* and *Arrabbiati* sometimes fought in the streets.

Savonarola thundered on. He attacked the priests for not living good lives, he attacked Rome, he attacked the Pope himself. Pope Alexander VI was not much bothered by these attacks. Priests and popes had been criticized before. What did bother him was Savonarola's politics. The French had been driven out of Italy, but they might make war again. Florence was allied with France, and the Pope believed Savonarola was responsible.

Savonarola continued preaching, accusing the clergy of being more interested in wealth than in goodness. Before Lent in 1497, the *Arrabbiati* planned a carnival. Savonarola's followers sent children around to all the houses. They collected "vanities"—carnival masks and fancy costumes, "immoral" pictures and books, playing cards and dice, love songs and musical instruments. The "vanities" were tossed into a huge pile and burned while church bells rang out.

At last the Pope excommunicated Savonarola, and the monk was silent for nine months. Then, sure that he was carrying out

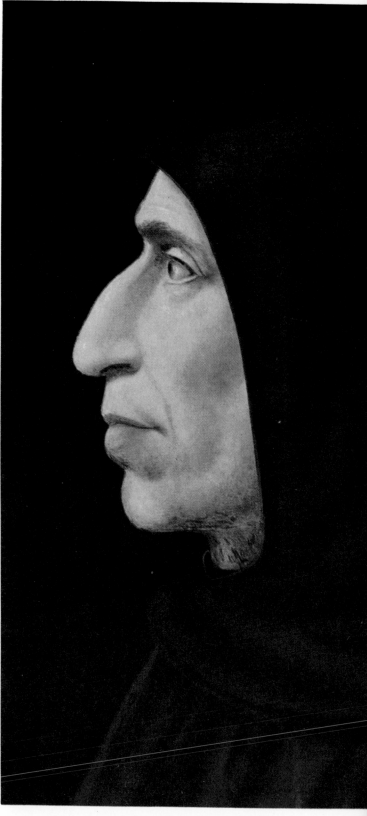

Savonarola's portrait was painted by Fra Bartolommeo, an artist who himself became a monk.

Savonarola and two of his followers were hanged and then burned in the great square of Florence.

the wishes of God, he began preaching again. "O Lord," he said, "if my deeds be not sincere, if my words be not inspired by Thee, strike me dead on this instant."

Savonarola was not struck dead, but not everyone was convinced that he was inspired by God. The Pope had a number of supporters in Florence, and among them were the Franciscan friars. A friar named Giuliano Rondinelli challenged Savonarola to the ordeal by fire. This was a test used during the Middle Ages, in which a person accused of a crime walked through fire. If he burned, he was guilty; if he was not harmed by the flames, he was innocent. Giuliano was willing to walk through fire with Savonarola. He believed they would both be burned, but at least Florence would be rid of an enemy of the Pope.

One of Savonarola's most faithful followers, a monk named Domenico da Pescia, volunteered for the ordeal, and a date was set. The ordeal took place in the Piazza della Signoria, a large public square, and all Florence turned out to see what would happen. When Domenico appeared in a red cape, the Franciscans protested. Savonarola might have put an enchantment on it to protect Domenico from the flames. Domenico changed his clothes, but rain and religious arguments between Savonarola and the Franciscans delayed the ordeal. Night came, and the Signory decided to stop the whole affair. The crowd felt cheated and turned against Savonarola. Fighting broke out between the *Piagnoni* and the *Arrabbiati*.

By this time, the members of the Signory had had enough of the disorder that threatened to ruin the city. They knew that as long as Savonarola lived, Florence would be divided. They ordered the arrest of the monk and his two closest followers. The three were tortured, and then condemned to die. Again a great crowd filled the Piazza della Signoria, and it was not cheated.

Savonarola was asked, "In what spirit do you bear this martyrdom?"

"The Lord has suffered as much for me," answered Savonarola, kissing the crucifix he held in his hands.

He and his two followers were hanged, and, as they swung from the gibbet, a fire was lighted under them.

An eyewitness wrote: "In a few hours they were burnt, their legs and arms gradually dropping off; part of their bodies remaining hanging to the chains, a quantity of stones were thrown to make them fall, as there was a fear of the people getting hold of them; and then the hangman and those whose business it was, hacked down the post and burnt it on the ground, bringing a lot of brushwood, and stirring the fire up over the dead bodies, so that the very least piece was consumed. Then they fetched carts, and accompanied by the mace-bearers, carried the last bit of dust to the Arno, by the Ponte Vecchio, in order that no remains should be found."

Later, the Medici returned to power. Some of them ruled well, some ruled badly, but the family went on collecting art. At last only one Medici was left, Anna Maria Ludovica. She died in 1743, and her will gave all of the family's treasures, its collections of art, its libraries, its palaces and buildings, to the citizens. On her tomb was inscribed, "Anna Maria Ludovica, last of the royal race of the Medici."

And so ended the family which had led Florence to greatness, and which, in the time of Lorenzo the Magnificent, had given the city a golden age of art and learning.

FLORENCE

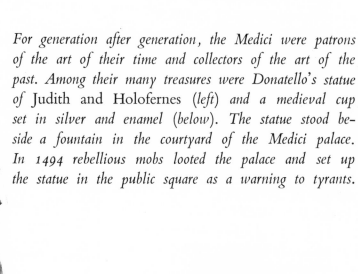

For generation after generation, the Medici were patrons of the art of their time and collectors of the art of the past. Among their many treasures were Donatello's statue of Judith and Holofernes (left) and a medieval cup set in silver and enamel (below). The statue stood beside a fountain in the courtyard of the Medici palace. In 1494 rebellious mobs looted the palace and set up the statue in the public square as a warning to tyrants.

OF THE MEDICI

The great dome of the cathedral of Florence, designed by Filippo Brunelleschi, was one of the most daring architectural feats of the Renaissance. It became the symbol of a city that welcomed art and learning. Under the rule of the Medici, until the death of Lorenzo the Magnificent in 1492, Florence attracted artists and scholars from all the countries of Europe.

In 1400, in spite of the plague which infested the city, the cloth merchants' guild of Florence decided to adorn the church of St. John the Baptist with another set of bronze doors. Seven artists competed for the commission, each submitting a sample panel of a Biblical scene. The competition was won by Lorenzo Ghiberti, a sculptor, painter, and goldsmith. "I had surpassed everyone," Ghiberti boasted, and, indeed, everyone agreed that he deserved the prize. It was twenty years before the doors were finished, and then the merchants were so pleased that they ordered another pair. Of this second set of doors (right), Michelangelo said that they were worthy to stand at the entrance to Paradise. Ghiberti modelled the panels according to the laws of perspective, so that, as he said, the figures "which are nearest are seen to be larger than those further off, just as happens in reality." He included his own portrait (above) twice in the decorative borders of the door.

Ghiberti planned his panels so that they would be "compositions rich with many figures." His success in carrying out his aim is shown in the Old Testament scene (above) of the sacrifice of Isaac. The squirrel (below) is a detail from the border.

SIC AVGVSTINVS SACRIS SE TRADIDIT VT NON
MVTATVM SIBI ADHVC SENSERIT ESSE LOCVM

Inventories of the Medici palace carefully described and valued each one of the family's precious possessions. The painting (above) by Fra Angelico and Fra Lippo Lippi, titled The Adoration of the Magi, was valued at a hundred florins.

The humanists who flocked to Florence tried to link the teachings of Christianity with the teachings of the Greek and Roman philosophers. The artist Sandro Botticelli painted Saint Augustine as a scholar in a typical humanist's study (left).

(Next page) On the chapel walls of the Medici palace, Benozzo Gozzoli painted the story of the journey of the Magi. Following the custom of the day, he included portraits of the Medici in his picture. Leading the procession, in golden robes and red hose, is a young man thought to be Lorenzo. After him comes Piero de' Medici, on a white horse, and Cosimo on a mule beside a Negro page. Well back in the crowd, between two bearded men, is Gozzoli's self-portrait, with his name written along the rim of his red hat.

63

MILAN, CITY OF STRIFE

Nature was kind to Milan. To the south lay the Apennine mountains, with an easy pass to the busy and wealthy seaport of Genoa. To the north and west rose another natural barrier, the Alps. The few passes that led to France or southern Germany gave Milan control of the routes from Genoa to the markets of the North. Between the mountains was the great plain of Lombardy, with the fertile valley of the Po River.

Perhaps nature was too kind to Milan. The walls of the mountains seemed to hold in the sunshine, and rich crops grew from the soil. Rich crops meant a large and prosperous population, and the plain was dotted with thriving cities. They included Turin, Pavia, Lodi, Brescia, Bergamo, Vicenza, Verona,

It took the rulers of Milan more than a century to finish constructing the city's cathedral, which at that time was the largest church in the world.

Padua, Ferrara, Bologna, Mantua, Parma, and Piacenza.

Here, if anywhere in Europe, was a natural place for a strong unified state. And yet the cities fought and plotted among themselves, acting together only in times of the greatest danger. And, within the cities, the merchants never succeeded in completely breaking the power of the aristocracy. Outsiders, too, were interested in gaining power or territory—the Holy Roman Emperor, the princes of Savoy, the French—and for a thousand years some of the bloodiest battles of Europe were fought on the plain. So the story of Milan was a story of war and feuds and strife. Important in the story were two families, the Visconti and the Sforza, and three dukes of Milan—Gian Galeazzo Visconti, Francesco Sforza, and Lodovico Sforza. Between them, they created a state as powerful and wealthy as Florence or Venice, and the story of Milan can best be told through them.

By the time Gian Galeazzo was born in 1351, the Visconti had played a leading part in the Lombardy region for more than two hundred years. His father, Galeazzo II, shared the Visconti lands with a brother, Bernabò. Galeazzo ruled in Pavia, while Bernabò ruled in Milan itself. Even in that cruel age, Bernabò was known as a cruel man. He taxed his people without mercy. He forced the peasants to take care of his 5,000 hunting dogs, and to keep them always in the best of condition. He punished crimes against the state with forty days of torture.

Galeazzo spent large sums of money on building churches and palaces, and was a patron of Petrarch, the greatest writer of the time. He also liked to marry his children to royalty. His son, Gian Galeazzo, was married to a French princess at the age of nine. When Galeazzo died in 1378, Gian Galeazzo inherited his father's lands. Highly intelligent, shrewd and cunning, he was determined not to share the Visconti lands with his uncle Bernabò. His wife had died, and he decided to better his position with a good marriage. He arranged to marry the daughter of the ruler of Sicily—a bargain that would be good only if the marriage took place within twelve months.

Bernabò, who had five ambitious sons of his own, was just as determined to win all the Visconti lands for himself. He made certain that his nephew would not be linked with the power of Sicily. Gian Galeazzo and his Sicilian bride never got within five hundred miles of each other. A year passed, the marriage was called off, and Gian Galeazzo agreed to marry Bernabò's daughter.

As a matter of fact, Gian Galeazzo agreed to almost anything Bernabò suggested. He tended to his own business, improving his government, reducing taxes, stopping dishonesty. He seemed a scholarly, timid, and religious man who would never be a threat to his uncle.

It was true enough that Gian Galeazzo was scholarly. He adorned his palace, looked after his great library, carried on discussions with scholars. It was also true that he was timid—but he was timid only in certain ways. While he lacked the courage to fight on the battlefield, he was daring in thought and spirit. He was not nearly as religious as he pretended to be. He had more faith in astrology and astrologers than in prayer and priests. And, when his astrologers told him that the time was right, he set out on a pilgrimage to the shrine at Varese.

The large bodyguard he took with him surprised no one, least of all Bernabò. Who did not know that Gian Galeazzo was timid? His travels brought him near Milan, but he did not enter the city—out of fear, Bernabò thought. With two of his sons, Bernabò rode out to meet him. Gian Galeazzo greeted his uncle and cousins affectionately. Then he signaled to his guards, who captured the three. Marching into the city, he announced that he was now the only ruler of Milan and the Visconti lands. The Milanese had had enough of Bernabò, and they cried, "Long live the Count, and down with the taxes!" Later Bernabò died in prison—it was rumored that he was poisoned—and Gian Galeazzo was indeed ruler of Milan.

With Bernabò out of the way, Gian Galeazzo turned his attention to governing Milan and winning new territory. He had no interest in seeking pleasure. According to Giovio, a historian of the day, he did not care for "the delights of hunting and hawking, nor games of dice nor the allurements of women, nor the tales of buffoons and jesters." Gian Galeazzo "was wont to give himself up to meditation during solitary walks, to hold discussions with those who were most experi-

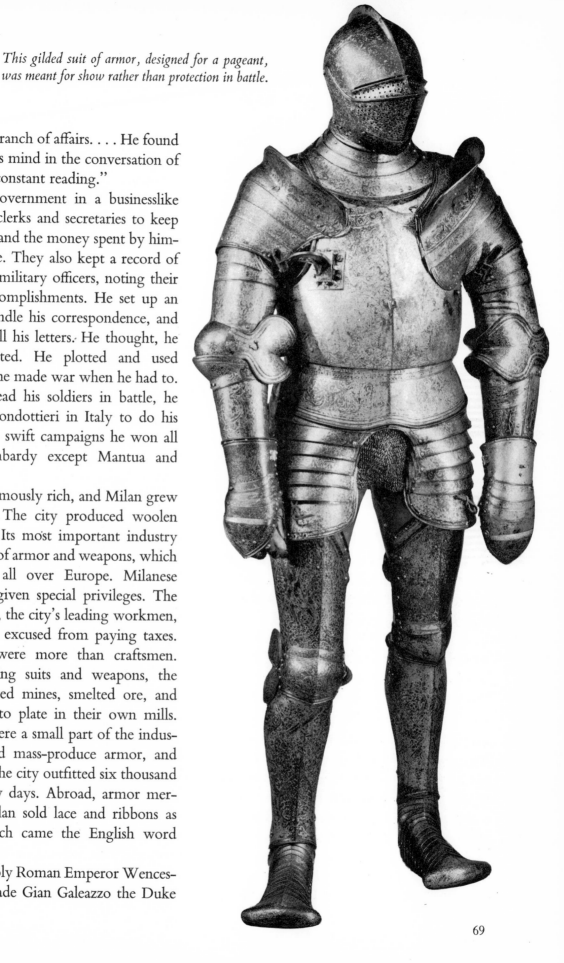

This gilded suit of armor, designed for a pageant, was meant for show rather than protection in battle.

enced in every branch of affairs. . . . He found relaxation for his mind in the conversation of scholars and in constant reading."

He ran his government in a businesslike way. He hired clerks and secretaries to keep records of taxes and the money spent by himself and the state. They also kept a record of his officials and military officers, noting their abilities and accomplishments. He set up an office just to handle his correspondence, and kept copies of all his letters. He thought, he planned, he acted. He plotted and used diplomacy, but he made war when he had to. Too timid to lead his soldiers in battle, he hired the best condottieri in Italy to do his fighting. In two swift campaigns he won all of eastern Lombardy except Mantua and Ferrara.

He grew enormously rich, and Milan grew rich with him. The city produced woolen goods and silk. Its most important industry was the making of armor and weapons, which were exported all over Europe. Milanese armorers were given special privileges. The Missaglia family, the city's leading workmen, were sometimes excused from paying taxes. The armorers were more than craftsmen. Besides fabricating suits and weapons, the Missaglia operated mines, smelted ore, and converted steel to plate in their own mills. Even so, they were a small part of the industry. Milan could mass-produce armor, and after one battle the city outfitted six thousand soldiers in a few days. Abroad, armor merchants from Milan sold lace and ribbons as well, from which came the English word *milliner*.

In 1395 the Holy Roman Emperor Wenceslaus officially made Gian Galeazzo the Duke

69

of Milan; he and his heirs were to rule the Duchy of Milan "forever." It cost Gian Galeazzo 100,000 florins, but he could well afford it. His income for one year was said to have been more than a million gold florins and perhaps as much as two million. He spent some of it on artists, poets, and scholars, some on buildings—he finished the castle at Pavia and began the cathedral at Milan—and some on the University of Pavia.

By 1402 he had won control of Pisa, Siena, Perugia, and Bologna. Only Florence stood between him and his ambition to establish a great northern Italian kingdom. The Florentines realized the danger and allied themselves with other cities against him. Nevertheless, he knew it was in his power to conquer Florence. He had built a state with a strong central government. He had good armies and well paid generals. He had wealth, and a mind that could think sharply and clearly. He might have conquered Florence, established kingdom, and changed the history of all Italy—if it had not been for the plague.

To escape the plague, Gian Galeazzo went to his fortress of Mariagnano. But there was no escape; he caught a fever. When he saw a comet flash across the sky, he believed it was a sign that he would soon die. "God could not but signalize the end of so supreme a ruler," he said. And he did die, at the age of fifty-one, and was cheated of his kingdom.

Gian Galeazzo's death all but broke up the state he had so carefully built. His oldest son, Gian Maria Visconti, who inherited his lands, was only thirteen, and a regency had to be set up. The generals and the aristocratic families fought among themselves for power. Milan lost many of the cities Gian Galeazzo had won, and again the plain of Lombardy was a place of blood and violence. Gian Maria had none of his father's ability. As he grew older, he became almost insanely cruel. It was said that

he fed his hounds on human flesh and enjoyed watching them tear men in pieces. This story was certainly untrue, but he was so cruel that the Milanese could easily believe it. His assassination in 1412 caused no surprise. Several nobles killed him in a church and threw his body into the street.

Gian Maria's place was taken by his brother, Filippo Maria Visconti. Filippo was fat and ugly, and sensitive about it. He never had his portrait painted and seldom appeared in public. He was so timid and nervous that he could not stand the sound of thunder. He had a chamber built with double walls to shut out the noise. He was superstitious as well, and was constantly consulting his astrologers. Ridiculous as he seemed, he turned out to be anything but ridiculous as a politician. He had inherited some of his father's ability to rule and to judge men. Also like his father, he helped scholars and artists.

By marrying the widow of a successful condottiere, Filippo received a large sum of money, soldiers, and some towns. Later he found an excuse to condemn the lady to death and took another wife. Filippo set himself the task of winning back the lost Visconti lands. Unable to fight, he had to hire condottieri, and among them was Francesco Sforza, the best general in Italy.

Francesco Sforza seemed born to be a soldier; he was the son and nephew of fighters. His father, Muzio, had been a substantial peasant. Running off with a band of wandering adventurers, Muzio became their leader and an outstanding condottiere. He fought well for Naples, but fell out with the queen and was jailed. His sister put on armor and freed him from his jailers. Muzio was then hired to command one of the Milanese armies, and was drowned while on a military mission. Francesco took his place and proved to be a great soldier. As hard and tough as he was tall

Milan was besieged forty-eight times. By 1472 it was heavily fortified and surrounded by a high wall.

and handsome, Francesco went about bare-headed in the cold of winter and the heat of summer. He was a master of military strategy and tactics, and a master of men. He could out-run, out-jump, and out-wrestle any of his troops, and he had their complete loyalty.

Filippo was suspicious of everyone around him, but he had good reason not to trust Francesco. Francesco was not satisfied with being a great general. He wanted riches, power, and territory of his own, and to get them he fought both for and against Milan. Filippo, meanwhile, was trying to win back and hold the Visconti lands. He badly needed Francesco, and at last he succeeded in arranging a marriage between Francesco and his daughter Bianca.

When Filippo died, the way was open for Francesco to make himself the Duke of Milan. But he happened to be away from Milan at

The assassination of Galeazzo Maria Sforza

the time, and the citizens took things in their own hands. They set up a republic. Unfortunately for the Milanese, neither Florence nor Venice liked the idea of a sister republic. They gave it no help, and its troubles multiplied until it crumbled. This was the moment Francesco had been waiting for. He entered the city, where the citizens went wild with delight. They rushed him and his horse into the cathedral, acclaiming him Duke of Milan.

Never had a condottiere won such a prize. Francesco established his court at Milan and ruled as he had led his troops—wisely, directly, decisively. He allied himself with other states, sometimes by marrying his children to the children of rulers. He kept the peace, and Milan prospered. At the edge of the city he built the Castello Sforzesco, a huge castle for protection against war or revolt. A citizen reminded him that princes should rely only on the love of their subjects for protection. Francesco felt that he could trust his people; nevertheless he fortified the castle.

He also built canals and a large hospital. The Ospedale Maggiore, or Great Hospital, was shaped like a cross so that patients could hear Mass being sung in the central chapel. He brought in artists and scholars, including the

humanist Filelfo, and became the father of twenty children. He died in 1466, and his enormous wealth and power went to his son, Galeazzo Maria Sforza.

Raised in luxury, Galeazzo was altogether different from his soldier father. He loved shows—tournaments, pageants, processions. He thought nothing of ordering a thousand or more costly velvet costumes for his servants. One of his pleasures was to take a visiting prince or ambassador to his jewel house, where rubies, emeralds, sapphires, and diamonds lay in heaps. On a visit to Florence in 1471, he was accompanied by two thousand courtiers on horseback, as well as bodyguards of soldiers and hundreds of hunting dogs and hawks. He also loved music, and searched Italy and Flanders for good singers.

More than shows, more than music, Galeazzo loved to display his personal power, and he did this in the most cruel manner. He was hated and feared, and in 1476 three young men and an old teacher plotted his death. Meeting in a garden, they rehearsed their crime, stabbing each other with sheathed daggers. On the morning of December 26, they prayed in Saint Stephen's Church, then waited for Galeazzo. When he entered the church, they immediately performed the scene they had rehearsed in the garden. They plunged their daggers into him. "Ah, God!" cried Galeazzo, and fell dead at their feet.

Two of the three assassins were killed at once. The third, Girolamo Olgiati, was captured and tortured. A priest asked him to repent. Olgiati answered: "As for the noble action for which I am about to die, it is this which gives my conscience peace; to this I trust for pardon from the Judge of all. Far from repenting, if I had to come ten times to life to die by these same torments, I should not hesitate to dedicate my blood and all my powers to an object so sublime."

And just before he died, as he was slowly and carefully torn to pieces, he murmured in Latin, "Death is bitter, fame endures."

Galeazzo had been killed before he could confess his sins, and his widow was deeply troubled. She made a list of his sins and was horrified. She wrote that he had been "versed in warfare, both lawful and unlawful; in pillage, robbery, and devastation of the country; in extortion of subjects; in negligence of justice; in injustice knowingly committed; in the imposition of new taxes which even included the clergy; in carnal vices; in notorious and scandalous simony and innumerable other crimes." Afraid that he would have to suffer long and terrible torments in Purgatory, she asked the aid of the Pope. The Pope granted Galeazzo absolution in return for a large sum of money for the papal army.

Galeazzo left a seven-year-old son, Gian Galeazzo, and five brothers. The boy was too young to rule, of course. A regent would have to rule for him until he was old enough to take on the duties of the head of the state. But who would be regent? A bitter struggle for power began. Milan and Italy itself were shaken by plots and schemes and conspiracies.

One of the five brothers was Lodovico, called *Il Moro*—the Moor—because of his dark hair and eyes. He tried to kidnap the child duke, but failed. Then he won the support of the Pope and King Ferrante of Naples. With good judgment, combined with good luck, he succeeded in making himself regent of Milan. He imprisoned the boy's mother, and chopped off the head of Cecco Simonetta, the ducal secretary. Simonetta had served the Sforza well throughout his long life, but he had tried to protect the young duke against the loss of all his inheritance. Fortunately for Lodovico, the most active and ambitious of his brothers had died during the struggle for power. Gian Galeazzo himself proved to be so weak in body, in character, and in intelligence that it was unnecessary to kill him off.

Lodovico had been educated by humanists, particularly by the famous scholar Filelfo. But his mother had told his teachers that "we have princes to educate, not merely scholars," and he had learned how to rule and how to make war. He was extremely intelligent and cunning. He knew that to hold his power he must make Milan prosperous. He knew, too, that to keep from being crushed by other states he must use diplomacy. He ruled with great ability and became one of the best diplomats of his day. He encouraged trade, manufacturing, and farming. He built canals. He set up an experimental farm and introduced new crops, such as rice. He employed Leonardo da Vinci not only as a painter and sculptor, but as an inventor and engineer. He established schools, and richly rewarded the artists, architects, scholars, philosophers, historians, poets, and musicians who came to the city.

He arranged a marriage between Gian Galeazzo and Isabella of Aragon. He arranged another between himself and Beatrice d'Este, the daughter of the Duke of Ferrara and the granddaughter of the King of Naples. Both marriages were arranged for political reasons; Beatrice d'Este was only five years old when she was betrothed. When she was sixteen, Lodovico set a date for the wedding. It would take place in Pavia on January 17, 1491.

Messengers from Milan began arriving in Ferrara. They brought gifts from Lodovico, such as the famous necklace of pearls with flowerets of gold and drops of rubies, pearls, and emeralds. Artists came, like Gian Cristoforo Romano, who carved a bust of Beatrice in marble. Masters of ceremony came, to prepare for the journey. They recommended that she bring with her many embroidered and bejeweled gowns.

S · LVDOVICVS

VTRIQ: TENEOR · DEDIT ILLE TV COSERV

PRM · F FPRM · PAITE VENER

In this fanciful painting, Lodovico Sforza kneels with his nephew, Gian Galeazzo, then Duke of Milan.

Beatrice and her attendants finally arrived in Pavia to find the city bleak with snow and cold. But inside Lodovico's castle, one of the grandest in the world, all was warmth, wealth, and luxury. Lodovico showed Beatrice through the castle's halls and chambers. Its greatest treasure was the library begun by Gian Galeazzo Visconti, to which the Sforza had added many illuminated volumes and copies of rare Greek and Latin manuscripts. Surrounded by so much splendor, Beatrice seemed meek and timid. The morning after the wedding, Lodovico left for Milan to see to the celebrations. A company of artists, headed by Leonardo da Vinci and Bramante, was already at work on all sorts of delights and surprises.

Later, Beatrice moved on to Milan, and the celebrations began. There were banquets, tournaments, masquerades, dances, theatricals, concerts, all of unbelievable magnificence. Men and women were dressed as gods and goddesses. Knights jousted in Moorish costume. The Street of the Armorers was lined with rows of empty suits of armor, looking like a regiment of warriors on parade. Wild men, in costumes designed by Leonardo da Vinci, gave the ladies a delicious fright. Dwarfs, giants, and hunchbacks capered. Poets turned out pages of verse for the occasion, musicians played and sang through the day and night, and fireworks flashed against the dark sky.

It was a fantastic show, and Beatrice was the heroine. She saw that her youth attracted Lodovico, and she no longer seemed meek or timid. She was gay, merry, charming, and lived in a whirl of amusements. She spent her hours, as a writer of the times said, "in singing and dancing and all manner of delights." She never grew tired of thinking up masquerades, jokes, or expeditions. Some mornings she, a friend, and Diodato the jester would set out in a carriage, singing. They fished, they lunched, they played ball and fished again. Lodovico was enchanted with the antics of his young wife, and laughed and applauded her.

Beatrice soon developed a taste for luxury. Eighty-four new dresses, heavily embroidered with gold thread, jewels and pearls, hung in one room. She had other rooms crammed with silver, ivories, precious glass, paintings, perfumes, lutes, clavichords—enough, as her mother said, to "fill all the shops." She became proud and commanding, and was often inconsiderate of the people around her. She played cruel little games, such as pretending to set her horses galloping at her terrified ladies-in-waiting. But she was still charming, and she was intelligent as well. She put her sharp mind at the service of her husband. She helped him in his diplomatic plots, and negotiated with princes and ambassadors.

Lodovico welcomed her help, for he wished to become Duke of Milan by law. He already had the power. Now he wanted the legal right to the title, so that it could be passed on to the son Beatrice gave him. Gian Galeazzo, too, had had a son. The birth had been celebrated modestly. But the birth of Lodovico's son was celebrated with banquets, jousts, and pageants, as if the infant were already heir to the title. Gian Galeazzo's wife, Isabella, was furious, and there was bad feeling.

The title of Duke of Milan could be granted only by the Holy Roman Emperor. Lodovico kept running to his astrologers, asking them the best time to take action. His chance came when Charles VIII of France decided to invade Naples. In return for Lodovico's promise not to fight against him, King Charles

Lodovico's emblem—a mulberry tree

supported his claim to the title. And then Lodovico had a real piece of luck. Gian Galeazzo, the Duke of Milan, died. Lodovico proclaimed Gian Galeazzo's infant son duke. As he expected, the Council of the city refused to hear of it. These were difficult times, Milan needed a strong man to govern it, and the Council begged Lodovico to take the title himself. He was happy to follow their wishes, and a short time later the Emperor Maximilian granted the title to him and to his direct heirs.

75

The building of the Certosa, a monastery, was begun by the Visconti and completed almost 250 years later.

King Charles' campaign against Naples proved successful. Charles made no secret of his wish to take Milan, and Lodovico realized that the French could be dangerous to him. With the title safely in his hands, Lodovico suddenly changed sides. When Charles was forced out of Italy, Lodovico was one of those who hurried him on his way. Then, at the right moment, he changed sides again.

And so Lodovico came to his best years. No one could doubt that he was truly the Duke of Milan. He boasted that the Pope was his chaplain, the Emperor his condottiere, Venice his chamberlain, and the King of France his courier. Milan was prosperous, and all was

going well. For Beatrice, however, something had gone wrong. Lodovico had fallen in love with a lady of the court and refused to give her up. Beatrice pretended to the court that she knew nothing of this. She laughed, she sang, she arranged, she commanded. On January 2, 1497, she held a ball in her apartment. Toward evening she became ill, and was carried to her bedchamber. At two o'clock that morning she gave birth to her third son. The child was born dead, and within an hour and a half Beatrice, too, was dead.

Dressed in a robe of gold, she was laid on a bier at the church of Santa Maria delle Grazie. A thousand torches and thousands upon thousands of candles flamed at her funeral. They could not brighten the darkness that seemed to surround Lodovico. A citizen of the city wrote that he "showed such grief as had never been known before in Milan." Lodovico mourned, and the people mourned with him. He had never been much interested in religion, but now he prayed and went to three Masses every day. He locked himself up alone for hours at a time and wept—wept for his lost wife, his lost years, and the sins that could not be undone.

With the death of Beatrice, Lodovico's good fortune left him. Death struck again, sending King Charles VIII to his grave. The new king of France, Louis XII, said it was a disgrace that Charles had never taken Milan, and claimed it for himself. The rulers of most of the Italian states were overjoyed that Louis had chosen Lodovico as his victim. They quickly threw their support to the French, whose troops marched on Milan.

Lodovico, disguised, journeyed to Innsbruck, hoping to get the aid of the Emperor Maximilian. The men he had left in charge of his armies did not put up much of a fight, and the French won Milan. His friend, Bernardino da Corte, gave up the heavily fortified Castello for a large bribe. "Since Judas there was no greater treason," Lodovico said.

The French soon made themselves unpopular with the Milanese. The people disliked the behavior of their conquerors and the taxes they were forced to pay. Lodovico hired some soldiers, the French withdrew to the Castello, and he was welcomed back to Milan. But he did not have enough money to pay his men. Betrayed by both his generals and his dissatisfied troops, he was captured while trying to escape in disguise.

King Louis ordered Lodovico to be brought to France, where he was held, first at one castle, then at another. Although he was a

Dukes of both the Visconti and the Sforza families are portrayed on this marble portal of the Certosa.

77

prisoner, he was allowed the freedom of the castle grounds. He was allowed books and visits from friends. But one day he hid himself in a wagonload of straw and tried to escape. He was hunted down in the woods by bloodhounds and thrown into a small, dark cell in the dungeon of the castle. He was allowed no freedom, no books, no visits from friends.

Perhaps he stared at the darkness, remembering the shining days when he had ruled Milan with Beatrice at his side, with poets, scholars, artists, and philosophers about them. Perhaps he remembered the great glittering festivals, the music, the dancing, the fireworks, the singing, and the laughter. An aging, white-haired man in his late fifties, he stared at the darkness—and in the darkness he died, on May 17, 1508.

It was not the end of the Sforza. Lodovico's son Massimiliano was brought back to rule Milan in 1512. Massimiliano's life had begun happily. At his birth in 1493, the bells of Milan had rung out for six days, while he lay under a golden quilt in a gilded cradle. The Emperor Maximilian gave permission for the boy to be named after him. But when Massimiliano was seven, Lodovico was overthrown. The boy was exiled to Innsbruck, where he was raised like a German and learned German ways.

To welcome him back on his return, the Milanese built triumphal arches. Rain drenched the decorations and the people, dampening their joy. At any rate, they soon found that they had little to be joyful about. Massimiliano taxed the citizens heavily and spent money foolishly. In three years the French army again came over the Alps, and Massimiliano was exiled.

When young Massimiliano Sforza was asked what he wanted most, he replied, "Not to go to school."

This miniature from one of Massimiliano's schoolbooks shows him riding through the streets of Milan.

In 1525 the Emperor Charles V chased out the French, after winning a battle outside Pavia. With this battle, the last hope of Milanese independence disappeared. In spite of its good location, in spite of its wealth and its rulers of ability, Milan as a state had never been as well established as Florence or Venice or even Naples. The reasons were not hard to see. The feudal nobles had never lost all their power. They constantly quarreled among themselves and were always ready to support any adventurer who would favor their personal ambitions. The merchants, who hated the nobles, were themselves divided and jealous of one another. Finally, Milan was surrounded by cities almost as powerful as itself. Each of these cities had rich, ambitious, jealous guilds of merchants. They could not decide whether they would gain more by following the leadership of a strong Milan or by taking advantage of its weakness. And so, in spite of the abilities of the Visconti and the Sforza, Milan remained a city of strife, and never reached true greatness.

79

TWO GIANTS OF THE RENAISSANCE

The Renaissance was an age of great artists, but two artists tower above the rest like giants—Leonardo da Vinci and Michelangelo. Their greatness lies not only in the quality of their art, but in their quality as men. They changed the position of the artist from that of a mere craftsman to that of the philosopher, the thinker, who gives the world a new vision of life.

Leonardo was as much a scientist as he was an artist. Indeed, he left few finished works of art—not one whole statue, about a dozen paintings, some fine anatomical and mechanical drawings. Never satisfied with what had been done before, he was always experimenting with new techniques, and many of his paintings were already ruined in his own day. No wonder that in his old age he was full of regrets for the wonderful things he had planned and never finished. On page after page of his notebooks, he scribbled: "Tell me if anything at all was done . . ."

But he left behind him his notebooks with thousands of sketches, with thousands of ideas in many fields of science—ideas that were far in advance of their time.

The self-portrait opposite is the only known likeness of Leonardo da Vinci. He made the drawing below to illustrate the statement in Vitruvius' book on architecture "that the measurements of a man are arranged by Nature thus . . . The span of a man's outstretched arms is equal to his height." The handwriting above the drawing is Leonardo's own. He was left-handed, and in his notebooks he used "mirror writing," which reads from right to left instead of from left to right.

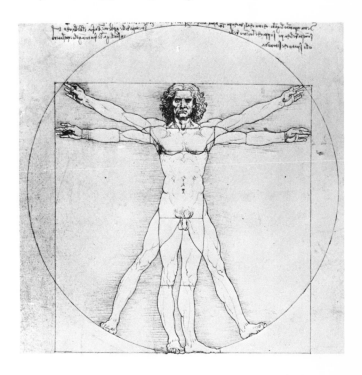

Whatever Leonardo observed, he recorded in his notebooks. About five thousand pages still survive, covered with drawings and comments on man, nature, and machines. Both the drawings and the quotations that follow are from his notebooks.

(1) Of this unborn child, Leonardo wrote that "the heart does not beat and it does not breathe because it lies continually in water. And if it were to breathe it would be drowned, and breathing is not necessary to it because it receives life and is nourished from the life and food of the mother."

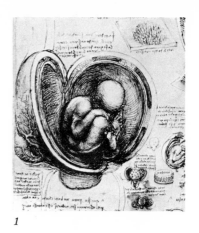

1

2

(2) Why study the shoulder? "The painter who has acquired a knowledge of the nature of the sinews, muscles, and tendons will know exactly in the movement of any limb how many and which of the sinews are the cause of it, and which muscle by its swelling the cause of this sinew's contracting, and which sinews having been changed into most delicate cartilage surround . . . the . . . muscle."

3

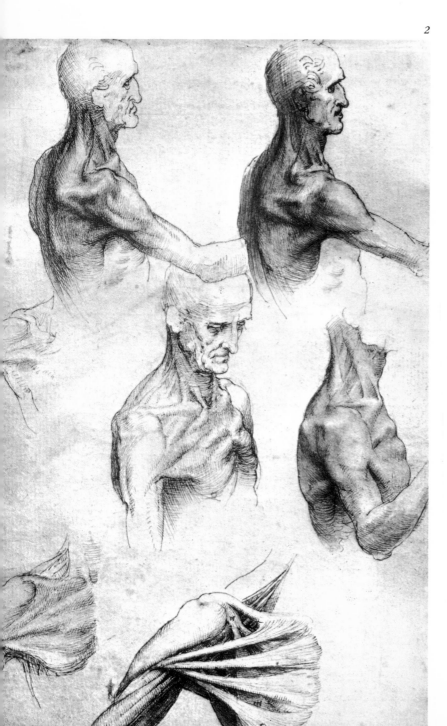

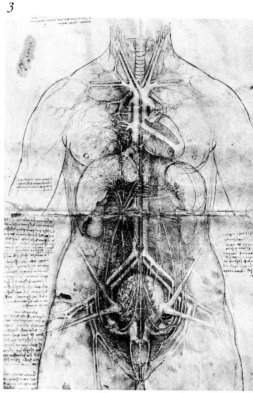

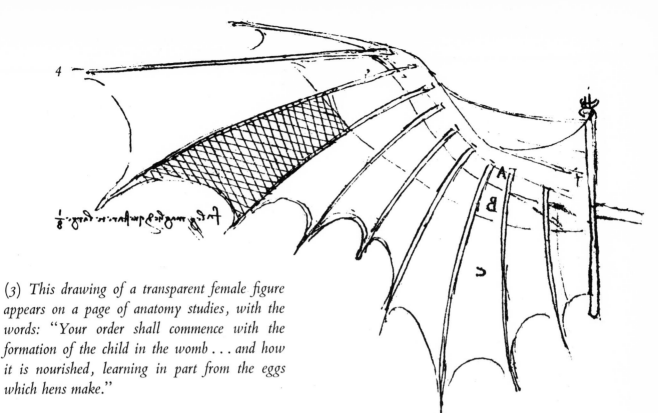

(3) *This drawing of a transparent female figure appears on a page of anatomy studies, with the words:* "*Your order shall commence with the formation of the child in the womb . . . and how it is nourished, learning in part from the eggs which hens make.*"

(4) *Leonardo believed that the painter must have a thorough knowledge of nature. At the same time, he delighted in* "*The imagining of things that are to be.*" *With this drawing of a wing mechanism came complete building instructions.* "*Make the meshes of this net one eighth wide. A should be of immature fir wood, light and possessing its bark. B should be fustian [a cotton and linen fabric] pasted there with a feather to prevent it from coming off easily. C should be starched taffeta, and as a test use thin pasteboard.*"

(5) *Long before modern aerodynamics, Leonardo designed the first parachute. He wrote:* "*If a man have a tent made of linen of which the apertures have all been stopped up, and it be twelve* braccia *across and twelve in depth, he will be able to throw himself down from any great height without sustaining any injury.*"

(6) *A machine, operated by man and lever, to demonstrate the lifting power of the wing.*

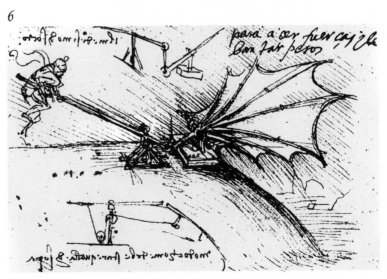

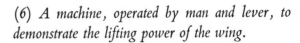

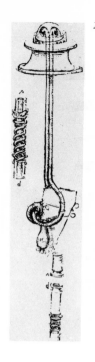

1

(1) *When Leonardo set down this design for a snorkel, he hinted that he had ideas for other submarine inventions:* "How and why I do not describe my method of remaining under water for as long a time as I can remain without food; and this I do not publish or divulge on account of the evil nature of men who would practice assassinations at the bottom of the seas, by breaking the ships in their lowest parts and sinking them together with the crews who are in them; and although I will furnish particulars of others, they are such as are not dangerous, for above the surface of the water emerges the mouth of the tube by which they draw in breath, supported on wineskins or pieces of cork."

2

3

4

5

(2) This dredge for marsh mud would save time, because "the instrument which conveys the earth up from below is always in the act of carrying it and never turns back."

(3) An automobile, powered by springs.

(4) In his design for a two-decker city, Leonardo combined architecture with city planning. "The high-level roads are not to be used by wagons or vehicles such as these, but are solely for the convenience of the gentlefolk. All carts and loads for the service and convenience of the common people should be confined to the low-level roads."

(5) Continuing the description of his plan for a city, Leonardo wrote: "At every arch there should be a spiral staircase; it should be round because in the corners of square ones nuisances are apt to be committed."

(6) A study from nature.

(7) With this drawing of a bramble, Leonardo proved his theory that "branches are found in two different positions: either opposite to each other or not opposite. If they are opposite to each other the center stem is not bent; if they are not opposite the center stem is bent."

(8) Leonardo's comments on the misfortunes of a crab: "When the crab has placed itself beneath the rock in order to catch the fish that entered underneath it, the wind came with ruinous downfall of the rocks, and these by rolling themselves down destroyed the crab."

6

7

8

Opposite is Michelangelo in his later years, as portrayed by one of his followers. Michelangelo himself cared little for portraiture and even less for landscape painting; he expressed himself through the human figure. In the red chalk drawings above, he shows the heroic struggles of Hercules.

At the age of thirteen Michelangelo Buonarroti was apprenticed to Domenico Ghirlandaio, a Florentine painter. But he soon turned to sculpture, after he had seen the antique statues in the garden of the Medici palace. Impressed by the boy's talent, Lorenzo the Magnificent took him into his household. For several years Michelangelo lived in the palace, studying at the school of sculpture that Lorenzo had set up. He ate at the same table as Lorenzo, listening to the talk of the humanist scholars who were Lorenzo's companions.

It was during this time that a fellow-student, Pietro Torrigiano, answered one of his gibes with a blow on the nose. The blow left Michelangelo with a broken nose which marked him for the rest of his life. It was during this time, too, that he heard the sermons of Savonarola, which predicted doom for Italy unless the people changed their sinful ways. The monk's terrible words also left their mark on Michelangelo. Until the day of his death he was haunted by a sense of the sinfulness of mankind, of the doom that might some day come as a judgment from heaven.

Stubborn, moody, bitter, sharp-tongued, short-tempered, he lived only for his art. Once, asked why he had not married, he said, "I have only too much of a wife in my art, and she has given me trouble enough. As to my children, they are the works that I shall leave; and if they are not worth much, they will at least live for some time."

87

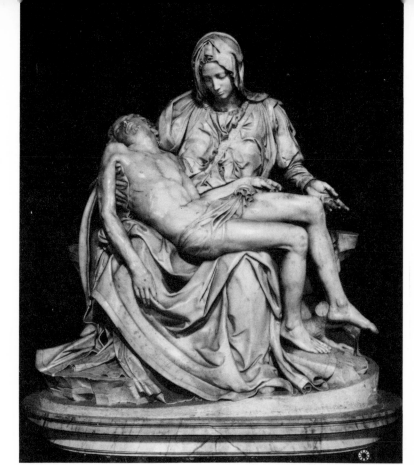

Michelangelo was young and little known when he carved the Pietà (right). It was the only work he ever signed; his name appears on the band across the Virgin's breast.

88

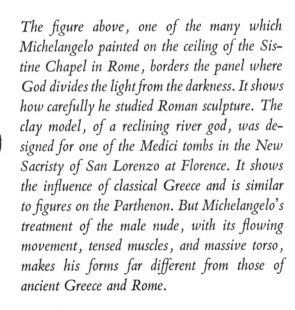

The figure above, one of the many which Michelangelo painted on the ceiling of the Sistine Chapel in Rome, borders the panel where God divides the light from the darkness. It shows how carefully he studied Roman sculpture. The clay model, of a reclining river god, was designed for one of the Medici tombs in the New Sacristy of San Lorenzo at Florence. It shows the influence of classical Greece and is similar to figures on the Parthenon. But Michelangelo's treatment of the male nude, with its flowing movement, tensed muscles, and massive torso, makes his forms far different from those of ancient Greece and Rome.

89

Like Leonardo da Vinci, Michelangelo was not satisfied with what he had accomplished. In a biography published shortly before his death at the age of eighty-nine, his pupil Ascanio Condivi wrote that he "was little contented with his works . . . his hand not appearing to carry out the ideas he has conceived in his mind." During the week in which he died, Michelangelo was working on the Rondanini Pietà (left). Also unfinished was a statue planned for the tomb of Julius II. Michelangelo and Pope Julius II had a deep respect for each other, but both were strong-willed men and they sometimes quarrelled. At first Michelangelo hesitated to accept the Pope's commission to decorate the ceiling of the Sistine Chapel with scenes from the Old Testament. "This is not my trade," he said; he was not a painter, but a sculptor. Yet he feared the power of the Pope and he could not afford to lose the fee of 3,000 ducats that he was offered. In 1508 he began the work of painting the ceiling, an area of ten thousand square feet, and finished it in 1512. Years later, in 1536, at the request of Pope Paul III, he painted his last and most famous fresco on the altar wall—the Last Judgement. The wall and the ceiling are shown at right; the paintings on the other walls are by Botticelli, Pinturicchio, and Perugino.

ROME, CITY OF POPES AND SPLENDOR

In 1400 Rome was like an old man lost in dreams and memories of a glorious past. No longer could the city boast of the proud title, *Roma caput mundi*—Rome, the world's ruler. Even the great days of the Middle Ages seemed far away, and gone forever. For the center of Rome was the pope, and during most of the fourteenth century the popes had lived at Avignon in France. To Avignon went the cardinals and courtiers—and to Avignon went the lawyers and merchants, the artists and scholars, to get their share of the wealth which a religious Europe poured into the laps of the popes.

While Avignon prospered, Rome was poor, miserable, and infested with the plague. Among the vast ruined buildings, many families—the Orsini, the Colonna, the Frangi-

pani and the others—fought and feuded. They tossed each other into the Tiber River, terrorized the citizens, robbed the monks, looted the churches.

Then, in 1377, the Papacy returned from Avignon with its cardinals and courtiers, its scholars and artists. But the Church became divided into rival groups, in the split that was called the Great Schism. From 1378 to 1417, there were two men who claimed to be the true pope; in 1409 there were even three. The broken-down streets of Rome were noisy with violence, riot, and rebellion. Popes and kings hired the toughest, most brutal condottieri. Among them was Braccio, who was said to enjoy the sufferings of others. For his pleasure he would throw a few men from the highest towers in Rome or drop a prisoner into a boiling cauldron. The flood of violence and brutality broke the government of the city in pieces, and it seemed as though the suffering of the people would never end.

One of the finest architectural achievements of Renaissance Rome is the Tempietto by Bramante.

NICHOLAS V (1447–1455)

PIUS II (1458–1464)

SIXTUS IV (1471–1484)

CLEMENT VII (1523–1534)

The Great Schism, which split the Church, ended in 1417, but not until 1471 were affairs fully under the control of Rome. At that time Sixtus IV, the first of the "political popes," was elected to the throne. In the years that followed, papal power rose steadily, reaching its high point during the golden age of Leo X. This period of papal magnificence ended with the sack of Rome in 1527.

No one could have predicted that Rome was about to be reborn. And yet, under the Renaissance popes, the glory of the ancient city was indeed reborn. Spacious palaces were built amid the decaying ruins. Churches rose, gardens were laid out, and wide avenues swept over crumbling temples and arches. Much of the new building was at the expense of the old. Pope Nicholas V removed 2,300 wagonloads of marble from the Colosseum in a single year. Sixtus IV destroyed the oldest bridge over the Tiber River and built a new one, also using masonry from the Colosseum.

For two hundred years the beauty of Rome became the pride of the Papacy. Each pope tried to outdo those who had come before him. The interiors of palaces were adorned with magnificent paintings, frescoes, and collections of antiquities. The greatest monument of all, however, was the new Basilica of St. Peter. The ancient church was ordered destroyed, and in 1506 Julius II laid the cornerstone for a new church designed by Bramante. The work of building went on slowly, and later popes hired other architects, each with a new plan or addition. Finally Michelangelo was put in charge. He returned to the original scheme, adding the great dome. He died before his work was completed, and the plans were changed again, but the great dome remained.

One of the reasons for beautifying Rome was to show the strength of the Church. And the Church badly needed to impress Europe with its strength. To be secure in Rome, the Papacy had to control the States of the

ALEXANDER VI (1492–1503) JULIUS II (1503–1513) LEO X (1513–1521)

Church which stretched diagonally across the long leg of Italy. During the Great Schism and the time the Papacy was at Avignon, the popes had lost many of their rights and privileges to various men and cities. What they had lost by force could only be won back by force. Indeed, it seemed to the popes that the Church could get back its own only by acting like any other ruling power in Italy. This meant the use of diplomacy and war. To be independent, the Church had to gain political strength. The popes had to be political leaders as well as religious leaders. They had to be worldly men—tough, hard-headed, ambitious, concerned with getting and holding power.

Like the princes of the Renaissance, the popes of the Renaissance knew that they could display their power with works of art. They were determined to build vast churches, huge palaces, magnificent fountains; to employ the best painters, sculptors, and craftsmen; to collect the loveliest antiquities, the finest jewels, the most remarkable books and manuscripts. These things, like armies, were necessities, and the cost was unimportant. And because the popes controlled more wealth than anyone else, the results in Rome were more splendid than anywhere else.

The dreadful split in the Church was cured, if not quite healed, in the time of Martin V, who was pope from 1417 to 1431. Martin proved to be a good administrator, and established peace in the city. He checked the robberies, violence, and murder, and encouraged trade. But the troubles of the Church were far from ended. During the rule of the next pope, Eugenius IV, the Colonna led a rebellion in the city. Disguised as a monk, Eugenius fled down the Tiber in a rowboat, and just managed to escape capture. He was forced to spend a number of years in Florence, where he was much influenced by the humanists. Meanwhile, a ferocious bishop named Vitelleschi restored order in Rome by slaughtering right and left. By 1443 Eugenius was able to return.

When Eugenius died, Nicholas V became pope—and it was Nicholas who brought the Renaissance to Rome. He had lived in Florence and had been friends with some of the leading humanists. He himself was a humanist as well as a Christian, and as pope he welcomed philosophers, poets, historians, grammarians, and teachers of Latin and Greek to the Vatican. More than anything else, Nicholas loved books. He sent agents to various countries to buy rare books and manuscripts. A small

The Roman Forum, once the center of an empire, was known for centuries as the Campo Vaccino, *or cow pasture.*

army of men was kept busy copying manuscripts he could not buy. He paid the highest prices for translations of the classics, offering ten thousand gold pieces for a translation of Homer's *Iliad* and *Odyssey*. He loved everything about books. He housed his library in the Vatican, and his books were handsomely bound in red velvet with silver clasps.

Nicholas also rebuilt and repaired many buildings and bridges. Some of this work was in preparation for the jubilee, or celebration, of 1450. That year thousands of pilgrims came crowding into Rome. They left behind them so much money, for both the merchants and the Church, that citizens of other towns said that all the gold was flowing into Rome.

96

Of the three popes who immediately followed Nicholas—Calixtus III, Pius II, and Paul II—the most notable was Pius II. He, too, was a humanist and a scholar. But he failed to unite Europe in a great crusade against the Turks.

Sixtus IV was the first of the so-called "political popes." There was no doubt that he was more of a political ruler than a religious leader. He stopped at nothing to get what he wanted, and gave his approval to the Pazzi conspiracy against Lorenzo the Magnificent. Born poor, he made up for it by living a life of extravagance and luxury when he was pope. He showered gold on his nephews, who were not at all backward about spending it.

Never since the days of the ancient emperors had Rome seen such feasts and festivities. A writer of the day described the banquet given by Sixtus for the daughter of the King of Naples:

"Before them were carried wild boars, roasted whole in their entire hides, bucks, goats, hares, rabbits, fish silvered over, peacocks with their feathers, pheasants, storks, cranes and stags; a bear in its skin, holding in its mouth a stick; countless were the tarts, jellies, candied fruits and sweetmeats. An artificial mountain was carried into the room, out of which stepped a liveryman with gestures of surprise at finding himself in the midst of such a gorgeous banquet; he repeated some verses and then vanished. Mythological figures served as covers to the viands placed on the table. The history of Atlas, of Perseus and Andromeda, the labors of Hercules, were depicted life size on silver dishes. Castles made of sweetmeats and filled with eatables were sacked and then thrown from the loggia of the hall to the applauding crowd. Sailing vessels discharged their cargoes of sugared almonds. . ."

Sixtus wanted Rome to have splendor as well as power. He widened streets, constructed bridges, built hospitals and churches. He gave land to all who would build houses and palaces. There was scarcely a section of the city that he did not improve in some way, but his greatest glory was the chapel in the Vatican that bears his name—the Sistine Chapel. To adorn the chapel, Sixtus brought the best artists in Italy to Rome. Among them were Signorelli, Botticelli, Perugino, Pinturicchio, Ghirlandaio, and Rosselli. There were so many painters in Rome during the 1470's that they formed their own guild.

Sixtus added 1,100 volumes to the Vatican library, and invited a number of humanist

The Apollo Belvedere *was one of the statues in the museum of antiquities begun by Pope Julius II.*

Pope Sixtus IV in the Vatican library

scholars to the city. To raise money, he sold the rights and privileges over which he had control. He said, "A pope needs only pen and ink to get what sum he wants." And a scholar of the day wrote, "Our churches, priests, altars, sacred rites, our prayers, our heavens, our very God, are purchasable."

Pope Innocent VIII, who followed Sixtus, carried on the same customs; in fact, he carried them further. To raise more money from selling appointments to office, he increased the number of offices. Criminals could buy pardons for their crimes, with the price depending on the seriousness of the crime. Rodrigo Borgia, who was a cardinal at this time, was once asked why criminals were allowed to go unpunished. He was reported to have answered: "God wishes not the death of a sinner, but rather that he should pay and live."

It was this same Rodrigo Borgia who became pope after Innocent, taking the name of Alexander VI. He was the strangest and perhaps the most interesting of all the Renaissance popes, and went down in history as a man of strong passions. He won his election to the Papacy by bribing the cardinals to vote for him with promises of privileges, rights, and lands. There was nothing new about this; it was a common practice during those times.

Alexander had had a number of children. His favorites were his daughter, Lucrezia, and his oldest son, Giovanni. On the night of June 14, 1497, Giovanni disappeared after having supper with his brother Cesare at the home of their mother. Later a boatman on the Tiber River said he had seen a body thrown into the water on that night. When asked why he had not reported it at once, he answered that he had seen "a hundred bodies in his day thrown into the water at the said spot, and no questions asked about them afterwards."

The Pope ordered the river dragged, and Giovanni's body was found with nine wounds in it. Evidently he had been stabbed before being thrown into the river. Just who the murderers were was never discovered, though some Romans suspected that Cesare was responsible.

Almost mad with grief, Alexander shut himself up in a room and refused to eat. His moans and howls were so loud that they were heard in the street outside the palace. At last he called a meeting of the cardinals. Weeping and tearing his robe, he told them that he had loved his son "more than anyone else in the world." Giovanni's death was God's way of punishing Alexander for his sins, and now he promised to "amend our life, and to reform the Church." He would sell no more offices or privileges, and he would no longer favor his own family. "We will begin the reform with ourselves," he said, "and so proceed through all ranks of the Church till the whole work is accomplished." And he appointed a committee of six cardinals to work out a plan of reform.

Melozzo da Forlì painted Pope Sixtus IV and four nephews receiving Platina, the new Vatican librarian. At the center stands the future Pope Julius II.

TEMPLA DOMVM EXPOSITIS·VICOS·FORA·MOENIA·PONTES:
VIRGINEAM·TRIVII·QVOD·REPARARIS·AQVAM·
PRISCA·LICET·NAVTIS·STATVAS·DARE·COMMODA·PORTVS:
ET·VATICANVM·CINGERE·SIXTE·IVGVM:
PLVS·TAMEN·VRBS·DEBET:NAM·QVAE·SQVALORE·LATEBAT:
CERNITVR·IN·CELEBRI·BIBLIOTHECA·LOCO·

A miniature showing Pope Alexander VI, who made his nephew Giovanni Borgia a cardinal.

But Alexander found that if he did not sell offices or privileges he could not raise enough money to support the Papacy. Besides, he wanted to build up the power of Rome, win back the lands that had been lost, and conquer still more. He soon forgot his promise to reform himself and the Church. Instead, he devoted himself to his new favorite, his son Cesare, and determined to create for him a great Italian kingdom.

Young Cesare already looked and acted like a king. He was strong and handsome. He was taller by a head than most tall men, and had huge shoulders. It was said that he could leap into the saddle without touching pommel or stirrups, and straighten the iron of a horseshoe with a twist of his wrist. Once he beheaded a bull with a single stroke of his sword. He was described as "a young man of great and surpassing cleverness and excellent disposition, cheerful, even merry, and always in good spirits."

Alexander made Cesare the commander of the Papal armies. He was not really a good general, or even a good combat leader. But, using treachery, bribery, and murder as well

as military force, he terrorized Italy. Once he put down a conspiracy against him by making peace with the four chief conspirators. Welcoming his enemies as friends, he invited them to a banquet, where they were seized by his bodyguards. Two of the men were neatly strangled on the spot; the other two were imprisoned and killed later. This deed made Cesare famous throughout Europe. A historian called it "a most lovely ruse," and King Louis XII of France said it was "worthy of the great days of Rome." Cesare himself said, "It is proper to snare those who are proving themselves past masters in the art of snaring others."

Aided at first by the French, he won great victories. Town after town fell into his hands. But once he was in full control of the land, he proved to be a just, if stern, ruler.

Alexander, too, ruled well. In 1501, at the age of seventy, he seemed satisfied with himself and his son. The Venetian ambassador, writing of the Pope, said that "nothing worries him" and "he seems to grow younger every day." Two years later, after dining together with other guests, both the Pope and Cesare became ill with malaria. While Cesare lay helpless in bed, the Pope died. The citizens of the city were glad to be rid of him. They rioted in the streets, burning and plundering houses.

The enemies of the Borgia were quick to take advantage of this opportunity, and there was little Cesare could do to stop them. He had been prepared for every emergency except this; he had never dreamed that he would be lying in a sickbed while his father died. Without a friendly pope he would lose his power, and he could not put his hands on enough money to buy the election. Luck was with him for a while. The cardinals elected a friendly pope, Pius III. But Pius died within a few weeks, and Cardinal Giuliano della

Rovere was elected pope, taking the name of Julius II. Julius was not at all friendly. Cesare was exiled to Spain, and finally, at the age of thirty-one, was killed in a brawl in Navarre. The power of the Borgia was ended forever.

The power of the Borgia was ended, but the scandalous stories about them were long remembered. Stories were told about Alexander, about Cesare, about Lucrezia. They left the impression that the favorite pastime of the Borgia had been poisoning their enemies. The stories about Lucrezia were almost certainly untrue. There was nothing remarkable about her except her cowlike disposition and long blond hair. The stories about Cesare were closer to the truth, though they must have been somewhat exaggerated. During his lifetime, it was a dull week in Rome when he was not suspected of murdering someone—by poison, by the hands of hired assassins, or by his own dagger. Probably he was really responsible for a fair share of the bodies hauled out of the Tiber River, and there is no doubt that he had the morals of a gangster.

As for Alexander, the Romans had always enjoyed spreading gossip and rumors about the popes. Alexander, however, gave them more excuse for juicy gossip than almost any other pope. Other popes had had children and had been immoral in their private lives. Other popes had sold high church offices, had been treacherous with their allies, and had used their position for the benefit of themselves and their families. But they had usually pretended to be doing something else. Alexander did not bother to pretend or to conceal anything. He seemed not to care what anyone thought about him.

There were even more important reasons for all the stories about him. Although he was far from a saint, he was an excellent administrator. He tried to control the territory around Rome as well as the city itself, and he tried to keep the Roman nobility in check. This made him unpopular with many Romans. He also tried to keep all the rights of the Papacy and to make sure of its rule over the Papal States. This made him unpopular with the ruling classes throughout Italy. Worst of all, perhaps, he was a foreigner, a Spaniard, and Italians had never liked a non-Italian pope. And so the Romans were willing to believe anything about him, and the stories spread.

Nevertheless, Alexander left the Papacy stronger than it had been in worldly power. Julius II, who became pope in 1503, was determined to make it even stronger. He hated the French and the great Roman families. His aim was to make the Papacy completely independent of emperors, kings, or Romans, and he never forgot his aim.

Sixty years old when he was elected pope, Julius was as active as a man of thirty. He loved war, loved to get on his horse, to feel the weight of his armor and hear the call of battle. He was not satisfied to let others fight his battles, but often commanded his armies himself. Even at the age of sixty-eight he led his soldiers in the siege of Mirandola, in spite of the winter's snow and cold. He had the spirit and manner of a soldier, and was never much for diplomacy. He said what he thought, and the older he grew the more outspoken he became.

In art as well as in politics, Julius knew what he wanted and went straight to the point. When he heard of the abilities of the young Raphael, he sent for him from Florence. He ordered that the paintings done by Piero della Francesca, Signorelli, Perugino, Sodoma, and other artists on the walls of certain rooms in the Vatican be whitewashed. Raphael was then to paint his own pictures on the walls. Raphael did as the Pope asked. The result was one of the great glories of Renaissance Rome, and the rooms became known as the Stanze of Raphael. Nor was this the only great work of art done during Julius' reign. He commissioned Michelangelo to paint the ceiling of the Sistine Chapel, and employed Donato d'Agnolo, known as Bramante, the most noted architect of the time, to design the new Basilica of St. Peter.

Julius died in 1513, and the next pope, Leo X, was different from him in almost every way. Julius had been sixty years old when he became pope; Leo was thirty-seven. Julius had been a man of war; Leo was a man of peace. Julius had been outspoken and straightforward; Leo was mild, courteous, even sweet in his manner, and could be a wily diplomat. Fat, bull-necked, pop-eyed, red-faced, Leo was a Medici, the son of Lorenzo the Magnificent. He loved luxury and he loved the arts, especially literature.

His coronation ceremonies gave the citizens of Rome a taste of what was in store for them. Not since the days of the emperors had the city seen such a gorgeous procession. Winding their way under triumphal arches, through streets adorned with emblems, inscriptions, and works of art, marched cardinals, bishops, priests, nobles from Florence and Venice, and representatives of Italy's great families—the Gonzaga, the Este, the Sforza, the Bentivoglio, the Colonna, the Orsini, the Baglioni. There were also chamberlains, standard-bearers, guards, attendants. Perspiring in the hot sun, dressed all in white, Leo rode side-saddle on a white horse. On that day no angry shouts were raised, no stones were hurled, no daggers flashed. The people had honored Julius at his death, and crowds had come to kiss the feet of the corpse. But they were tired of war, and they welcomed a pope who promised to be less ferocious.

Leo did not disappoint them. When he was made pope, he was supposed to have said, "Let us enjoy the papacy, since God has given it to us." He did enjoy it, and he shared his enjoyment with the people. For the ordinary citizen, there were festivals, pageants, and processions; for the learned, there was every kind of encouragement, including rich rewards of money. Leo employed the best painters and sculptors, among them Raphael and Michelangelo. He welcomed scholars, even those who were critical of the Papacy, and he surrounded himself with poets. He sponsored the study of Hebrew and Greek, bought rare manuscripts for the Vatican library, ordered splendid tapestries for the Sistine Chapel. The city was alive with gayety and learning, and sometimes the air seemed to crackle with the witty remarks of wise or clever men.

Art, literature, scholarship, music—Leo liked them all. When he took his meals he listened to music, or had a book read to him. He liked other kinds of amusement, too. His favorite sport was hunting, and he had a hundred grooms to care for the horses in his large stables. Always he kept jesters and buffoons about him, to entertain him with jokes or with ridiculous feats, such as eating forty eggs at one sitting.

Under Leo, Rome prospered and knew its Golden Age. But the times were not free from trouble. The power of the pope was still being challenged by the French, the Spanish, the Milanese, and the Venetians, and sometimes the peace was broken by violence or war. Besides, the splendor that Leo brought to Rome took money. He borrowed huge sums, raised taxes, and, like the popes before him, sold indulgences for sins.

When Leo died of a fever in 1521, the historian Paolo Giovio wrote, "Knowledge, art, the common well-being, the joy of living—in a word, all good things—have gone down into the grave with Leo." This may have been an exaggeration, but one thing was certain—never again would Rome have a patron of art and literature like Leo. In fact, he had spent so much money that he died owing vast sums to a number of bankers and cardinals. And in the enjoyment of the arts, he had neglected some of his duties. He had done nothing to reform the Church, and reform was necessary if Catholicism was to survive. Already, in Germany, Martin Luther was leading a revolt against the Papacy, a revolt that would end with the establishment of Protestantism.

Leo left behind him a confused and disturbed city. The cardinals were divided politically. Some supported Francis I, who was now king of France; others supported Charles V, the Germanic emperor. They elected Adrian VI, a Dutchman, to the Papacy. He was the first Teuton to become pope since 1161. Adrian had never been in Rome, knew no Italian, and spoke Latin with a strange accent. An eyewitness reported that at the news of his election the "courtiers of the Vatican and chief officers of the Church wept and screamed and cursed and gave themselves up to despair." The cardinals were accused of surrendering "the fair Vatican to a German's fury" and for a while they were afraid to appear in public.

Adrian was a simple, honest man who could not understand the Romans or the Renaissance. He had only two personal servants, to whom he gave one ducat a day for household expenses. A Flemish serving woman cooked his meals, made his bed, and washed his clothes. He kept only four of the hundred grooms who had looked after the horses in Leo's stable. Adrian did his best to bring about reforms in the Church. But he died in little more than a year after he was elected, and Clement VII became pope.

A Medici, Clement was a lover of the arts, and Romans looked forward to another happy time. They soon realized that they were mistaken. Clement found it hard to make up his mind about anything, and he was faced with many important decisions. The Turks were in Hungary; more and more people were joining Luther's revolt. King Francis and the Emperor Charles were at war, and Clement had to decide which to support. He finally allied himself with Francis, and signed a secret treaty with the French. When Charles learned of it, he said, "I shall go into Italy and revenge myself on those who have injured me, especially on that poltroon the Pope."

Raphael's portrait of the energetic Pope Julius II was said to be so realistic that "it seems alive."

This painting, probably by Pieter Brueghel the Elder, shows German and Spanish troops attacking Rome.

In 1527 Charles made good his threat. Reaching Rome, his soldiers broke into the city under the cover of fog. Many of them were Lutherans. They believed that the city's wealth had come from milking Christian nations dry, and they remembered Luther had said that "if there is a hell, then Rome is built on it." They sacked the city, slaughtering hospital patients, stabling their horses in shrines, kindling fires with precious manuscripts. They forced the Romans to pay ransoms for their lives. They killed and tortured and destroyed books and works of art. Thousands of men, women, and children died. Pope Clement was imprisoned in Castel Sant' Angelo. He let his hair grow as a sign of

104

The largest contingent storms the palace of the popes, the building with twin towers at upper right.

mourning, and roamed about, repeating Job's lament to God: "Wherefore then hast thou brought me forth out of the womb?"

When he was restored to power, only one-fifth of the city's houses were occupied. Diplomats forced the Emperor to give up his idea of stripping the popes of all their worldly power. Soon the Papacy was as splendid as ever, and Rome was rebuilt. For centuries the city would continue to grow in beauty, but the humanists had fled and would not return. Clement was the last of the Renaissance popes. The popes who followed him were strict and stern men, concerned with reforming the Church and strengthening Catholicism. Rome was entering a new age.

TREASURES OF THE VATICAN

The Popes of the Renaissance were among the greatest patrons of art in history. They commissioned hundreds of paintings, statues, tombs, and monuments, and in the Vatican are masterpieces by the dozens of Renaissance artists who worked there. One of these artists was Leonardo da Vinci, who, however, accomplished little during his short stay in Rome. His unfinished Saint Jerome (right) is therefore one of the prized possessions of the Vatican today. The fresco at left is by Fra Angelico, who painted scenes from the life of St. Lawrence for the private chapel of Pope Nicholas V.

The frescoes in the Vatican Stanze, or rooms, of Raphael represent the ideal combination of pagan and Christian themes in art. In the School of Athens (above) a number of pagan philosophers and scientists, led by Plato and Aristotle (center), discuss their ideas. On the opposite wall of the room is the Disputation on the Sacrament, representing the triumph of the Church Militant. The detail at right shows part of the assembly of saints and churchmen. Toward the end of his short life, Raphael undertook so many commissions that he had to assign much of his work to assistants. The fantastic mask at left is by Giovanni da Udine, who covered the arches and pilasters of the Logge with colorful stucco reliefs.

(Next page) On the wall of the Sistine Chapel is Botticelli's Punishment of Korah, Dathan and Abiram. At the center, Moses calls down the wrath of God on the rebels against his authority. At left, he sees them swallowed up by an abyss.

To paint the ceiling of the Sistine Chapel, Michelangelo had to spend many hours lying on his back on a scaffold. Pope Julius II threatened to throw him off the scaffold

unless he speeded up the work, and finally whacked him with his cane. But the
work could not be hurried, and it still took four years to complete the huge ceiling.

VENICE, THE CITY OF THE SEA

A poet once said of Venice, "The sea's the street there." And, indeed, the Grand Canal curved through the city like a broad street, a flowing roadway, a boulevard of water. Besides the Grand Canal, there were many smaller canals. The city was built on more than a hundred islands, and leaping from island to island, spanning the canals, were four hundred bridges. Venetians traveled, not by horse and carriage, but by boat. They lived surrounded by water, by the babble and murmur of water, and by the damp and smell that water brings.

Venice belonged to the sea, a fact that

Overlooking the Piazza of Venice are the bronze horses atop the Basilica of St. Mark and the two giants striking the hours upon a Renaissance clock tower.

Venetians celebrated with a strange ceremony. Every year, on Ascension Day, for eight hundred years, the ceremony was repeated. The huge state barge, the *Bucentaur*, carved and painted and gilded, set off from the Doge's Palace to the chants of choirs. Aboard the barge, under a canopy of crimson and gold, sat the Doge, the head of the Venetian government, on a high throne. Other government officials, nobles, and ambassadors from foreign lands followed in gilded gondolas, which trailed long lengths of velvet kept afloat by corks. Church bells rang, cannon fired salutes, musicians played, as the boats glided to the Porto di Lido. There the Doge stood up, cast a golden ring into the waters, and said, "O sea, we wed thee in sign of our true and everlasting dominion."

115

Venice in 1500. Neptune guards the entrance to the S-shaped Grand Canal, spanned by the Rialto bridge.

There was a good reason for the strange ceremony. The wealth of Venice came from the sea, or rather from ships that sailed the sea, linking the city with the East. Thanks to its ships, Venice was rich, powerful—and secure. Only twice in its history did enemy vessels sail into the waters of the Venetian lagoon, and both times the enemy was destroyed. To the landward, the city's defenses proved equally strong.

The Venetians made their ships in the great Arsenal that was one of the wonders of the Renaissance world. With its two thousand workers, the Arsenal was probably the largest industry of its time. Its great sheds extended over sixty acres, protected by two miles of

116

sails, oars, stores, and weapons. More important, almost everything was standardized. Replacements could be stored in all Venetian warehouses, even those in foreign lands, and could be used on any Venetian ship. Any crew could be moved to any ship without further training, or a fresh crew could be made up from survivors in battle. And every galley, whether a merchant ship or a warship, belonged to the state. No noble, even the most wealthy, could own a Venetian galley.

Such control gave Venice an enormous advantage over its rivals and made it hated by other sea powers. Genoa ruined itself trying to crush Venice in a long, hard war. By 1400 Venice had become the center of an empire. The city-state owned Zara, Ragusa, Crete, and many Aegean Islands. Trading communities, which had many special privileges, had been established in Constantinople, Acre, Tyre, Sidon, and Alexandria. Venetian merchants were as familiar with the Black Sea as with the Adriatic. Venetian travelers reached Sumatra and Ceylon long before Vasco da Gama rounded the Cape of Good Hope.

In Venice itself, Christians, Jews, Moslems, Greeks, and Armenians crowded the busy wharves, bargaining for the rich cargoes from the Orient. The Germans had a vast storehouse on the Grand Canal; the Turks had another. Venice had the earliest Jewish ghetto in Europe, and for centuries allowed the Armenians to follow their religion without fear. All the nations of Europe mingled with the races of the Near East. They were brought together by the simple fact that Venice was the greatest market of the Western world. Anything could be bought and sold in Venice. The chief trade, however, was in luxuries— spices, slaves, gold, silver, glass, silks, jewels. Throughout the barbarian times, when Venice grew to greatness, Europe lacked the skills and crafts already known in the Eastern Empire,

fortifications. Its shipwrights could build and repair more than a hundred galleys at a time, and at an amazing speed. A new galley was produced every hundred days.

Ships were fitted out by a method surprisingly like the modern conveyer-belt system. Moving past a line of storehouses, each vessel was quickly loaded with masts,

117

or in Syria and Egypt. In return for products from these places, Venice could offer the cheap raw materials that a primitive Europe produced—hides and tin from England, fine cloth from Flanders, raw silver from Bohemia, copper and steel from Germany.

And then there were the pilgrims. Century after century, in peace or in war, rich and religious Christians won their way to heaven by visiting the Holy Places—to the great profit of the Venetians. For centuries the Crusaders made war in the Eastern lands, and the Crusaders paid. They paid for themselves, their armies, their horses, their necessities, and the Venetians saw to it that they paid well.

In spite of wars against the Genoese, the Greeks, and the Turks, Venice grew rich. The production of luxury goods was encouraged. Venetian jewelers were the best in Europe during the Middle Ages, and kings sent to them for their crosses and scepters. The manufacture of glass, based on secrets learned from the East, was controlled by the government. So was the making of mosaic, which was practiced nowhere else in Europe.

The center of Venice's business life was the section called the Rialto, where Venetians had first settled in the ninth century. Here under the porticoes sat the merchants, shielded from the weather. Their wines, spices, and precious Eastern silks were displayed for sale in warehouses nearby. Along the quays before them, hucksters peddled fruit and fish. Overlooking the Rialto bridge was Europe's busiest money market, ready to serve the hundreds of foreign merchants who flocked to the city. Painted on a wall was a great map that showed the major routes of Venetian commerce, and on the walls of the Rialto parish church was written

118

The Doge's barge, the Bucentaur, *as depicted in a sixteenth-century souvenir book of Venetian scenes.*

this warning: "Let the merchant's law be just, his weight true, his covenants faithful."

The merchants of Venice were cautious and careful. They spread their risks, buying shares in several business ventures to lessen the danger from shipwreck, pirates, or the Turks. The more daring bid at auction to rent one of the state-owned ships that sailed in fleets across the Mediterranean. If all went well, a shipload of luxury goods could return a profit as high as forty per cent.

The center of another part of Venetian life was the Piazzo San Marco. Standing at one end of the vast square was the Cathedral of St. Mark, with its domes, its arched doorways, and its golden mosaics. High above the central doorway were the symbols of the state—four bronze horses and the winged lion of St. Mark. To the right of the cathedral was the pink and white Doge's Palace. During the Renaissance, many of the Piazza's eyesores—the fish market opposite the Doge's Palace, the barbers' and dentists' shops huddled around it—were cleared away and replaced by more splendid buildings.

The Piazza was the place of ceremonies, pageants, processions. Across the square, as if on a great stage, guilds and religious brotherhoods paraded before the Doge. They carried banners, jeweled boxes containing religious relics, and censers that perfumed the salt air with incense. In the Piazza each new Doge celebrated his election, scattering coins to the cheering crowd as he was carried past by a band of Arsenal workers.

The pageantry of Venice was famous and attracted crowds of tourists. Each May a hundred thousand visitors came to attend the springtime trading fair and to watch the ceremony in which the Doge married the Adriatic Sea. Others came for the annual carnival, to stroll the streets in masks and laugh at the actors performing in the piazzas. There was always something to see—the galleys decked with flowers, the dance pavilions floating on the Grand Canal, the regattas with boats rowed by beautifully dressed women. And there was always the city itself, the rich, splendid, dazzling city rising from the waters like a fantastic dream.

It was a city like a dream—but a highly organized dream, tightly controlled by hard-headed, hatchet-faced merchants. Although the Doge was the head of the government, the real power was in the hands of the Council of Ten. The Council shared some of its power with the Collegio, the heads of government departments. Below these were the Signory, or Senate, from which the members of the Council of Ten and the Collegio were appointed. Below the Senate was the Maggior Consiglio, or Greater Council, which appointed senators from its own members.

Venice called itself a republic, and so it was until 1297. In that year came the decree that no one could be a member of any of the ruling bodies unless his ancestor had been a member of the Greater Council between 1172 and 1297. To make sure of this, in 1319 the government began recording births and marriages of the privileged group in the Libro d'Oro, or Golden Book. The result was that the majority of Venetians lost all their political rights. A city of more than a hundred thousand persons was ruled by about a thousand aristocrats.

Not that the aristocrats lived a life of leisure. They were expected to officer the fleets, to take part in trade, to help govern the city's distant possessions. Above all, they had to be loyal to the state, which was more important than any individual.

Only an aristocrat could be elected Doge by the Senate, but the actions of the Doge himself were limited by laws and rules. An aristocrat offered the Dogeship was forbidden to refuse it. Once elected, he could not travel outside Venice. Neither he nor his sons could marry foreigners without permission. Neither his sons nor his personal officers could hold public positions under him, except as ambassadors or naval commanders. His income and his expenses were set by law. He could not choose his official councilors. He could not resign without the consent of his councilors and the approval of the Greater Council.

Aristocrats, merchants, craftsmen—all were forced to bow to the power of the state. Craftsmen who made glass were forbidden to use their skills in another country. If a craftsman did go to another country, his nearest relatives might be imprisoned. If he still refused to return to Venice, "secret measures" might be taken to have him killed wherever he might be. The Church, too, bowed to the power of the state. No man could be a bishop or even a parish priest in Venice unless he was a born Venetian.

The Council of Ten watched the citizens of Venice carefully and wanted to know everything about them. Throughout the city, there were receptacles in the shape of a lion's head.

Anonymous letters were dropped in the lion's mouth.

Gentile Bellini painted this religious procession, which is crossing the Piazza in front of St. Mark's.

Venice's colorful pageantry was famous, and visitors came from afar to see the sights of the dazzling city.

123

Venetians who were suspicious of their neighbor's loyalty could drop letters of information into the lions' mouths. The letters were not signed, but the Ten acted swiftly on the anonymous information. They acted silently, too, for no public trials were held in Venice. If a suspected person was found guilty, he was usually strangled in the dungeons, quietly and efficiently. Sometimes, however, other methods of punishment were used. A prisoner might be thrown into a part of the lagoon reserved for this purpose, where no fishing was allowed; or hanged by one leg from the pillars of the Doge's Palace; or cut in quarters and distributed about the city; or beheaded as a public spectacle.

Because its trade was so widespread, Venice needed to know the intentions of the Shah of Persia, the Count of Flanders, the Sultan of Cairo, the King of France, and the Duke of Ferrara. Ambassadors were sent to distant lands, and every merchant, every priest, was expected to spy for the good of his country. The Senate knew at once the deepest secrets of the most carefully guarded meetings of the Papacy, for the bishops of Venice put loyalty to the state higher than the command of the Church. Venetians in London, Paris, or Bruges sent home long, reliable, and beautifully written reports. They can still be studied today by historians who want facts on England, France, and the Netherlands as well as on Venice. In the building of the Archivio Centrale, next to the Frari Church, are a quarter of a million books, documents, and parchments—the greatest collection of its kind ever accumulated by a single city. And the reason it was accumulated is that the Council of Ten believed in knowledge, in information, in facts, no matter how unimportant they might seem.

Protected by this knowledge and the strict control of its own citizens, protected from attack by the lagoon, the rulers of Venice felt safe and secure. During the Middle Ages they scarcely thought of their city as part of Italy. They belonged to the sea, and the sea linked them to the East, to Byzantium and the Greek Emperor. But as their trade grew, they began to turn their attention to the mainland. They had to be certain of an outlet to northern Europe for the goods they brought in from the East. Besides, Venice owned no territory that produced grain and meat. There was always the danger that they might be cut off from their food supply by a blockade and starved into defeat.

So long as the Lombardy plain was divided among many small powers, Venice had little to fear. Then, in the fourteenth century, the small city-states of Italy began to fall to the rising power of Milan, Florence, Rome, and Naples. The danger was brought home to the Venetians when the lord of Padua joined with the Genoese to carry a war to the lagoon itself. The Venetians saved themselves by winning the great battle of Chioggia, but they no longer felt safe. They realized that they belonged to Italy as well as to the sea. And if they wanted to be a power in Italy, they needed more land than a few muddy islands and river mouths in a shallow lagoon. The Venetians were forced to turn their attention to the mainland, and they were drawn into Italian politics and war. They were successful in battle, and won control of Padua, Vicenza, Verona, and other cities.

Even so, some Venetians did not trust this policy. Becoming a land power had brought the city new problems. Land wars were costly. They kept the city from tending to its real business in the East. They created a new class of landed nobility and made the city depend on condottieri. In other Italian cities, new princes were rising from the landed nobility and condottieri, overthrowing the old rulers and becoming tyrants. The same thing could happen in Venice.

Among the Venetians who were fearful of the future was the Doge Tommaso Mocenigo. In 1423, as he lay dying, he sent for his councilors. When they had gathered at his bedside, he made a famous speech. The land wars, he said, would ruin the city's finances. The wealth of Venice came from trade, manufacturing, and shipping. To remain wealthy, these were the things Venetians must concern themselves with. The city needed peace, not war. Mocenigo warned that the next doge must be chosen with care, and went down the list of possible candidates. They were all members of the great merchant families, and there was something to be said for each of them. But at the end he warned them against one man—Francesco Foscari. Foscari was proud and ambitious. If he were elected doge, it would mean war, war, war. . . .

Why had the dying Doge spoken out so strongly against Foscari? To Mocenigo and his friends, Foscari was an outsider. He was not a member of a great family, but one of the "poor nobles." In fact, he was the leader of the lesser noblemen, who favored war by land. Furthermore he was only fifty years old, the youngest of all the candidates, and he was determined to be doge. True, the power of the doge was limited by law. But a skillful politician might know how to get around the law and set himself up as ruler. He might establish his family as the ruling power, as the Visconti had already done in Milan and the Medici were about to do in Florence.

Foscari soon proved that he was indeed a skillful politician. He out-maneuvered his rival, Pietro Loredan, and was elected doge. For a year he dazzled the city with feasts and pageants, then settled down to the serious business of government.

Foscari's reign, the longest of any doge in the history of Venice, was a time of splendor. New palaces, both public and private, rose by the Grand Canal and the lagoon. The Rialto bridge was rebuilt. Famous visitors were received with glittering ceremony. In 1428 it was the Prince of Portugal. The *Bucentaur*, escorted by a fleet of boats, brought him to a banquet attended by two hundred and fifty ladies in cloth of gold and silk and jewels. In 1438 it was the Emperor of Byzantium. When the *Bucentaur*, covered with red silk and golden emblems, carried the Emperor's party from the Lido, the lagoon was full of boats flying banners, with musicians playing music and oarsmen dressed in cloth of gold. In 1452 the Holy Roman Emperor was welcomed with an even more magnificent show.

Foscari's reign was a time of splendor, but it was also—as Mocenigo had predicted—a time of war. War for land went on almost constantly for thirty years. It was an expensive war, costing seven million ducats for the first ten years alone. Venice was not always victorious, and twice Foscari tried to resign. Each time he was reminded of the law and was refused permission to give up the office. In the end, however, Venice was again successful, and its territory extended far to the west.

A time of splendor, a time of war . . . and, for the Doge Francesco Foscari, a time of hatred and enmity. He had defeated the Loredan family in 1423, when he had been elected doge over Pietro Loredan. The Loredans never forgot their defeat. With their allies, the Dona and the Barbarigo families, they struck at Foscari through his son, Jacopo.

Foscari had had five sons, but four had died young of the plague. He was devoted to Jacopo, who was a Greek scholar and a collector of manuscripts. In 1441 Jacopo's marriage to Lucrezia Contarini was celebrated with a magnificent festival, in a city adorned

The Foscari villa, designed by Andrea Palladio

with scarlet and cloth of gold. There were boat races, feasts, illuminations, and a great tournament before thirty thousand people in the Piazza. Two hundred and fifty horsemen rode in cavalcade over the Grand Canal on a specially built bridge of barges.

Four years later, Jacopo was accused of secretly taking gifts from Filippo Maria Visconti, the Duke of Milan and an enemy of Venice. At that time Francesco Loredan, a nephew of the defeated Pietro, was one of the three chiefs of the Council of Ten. Ermolao Donà was another. The Ten arrested Jacopo, confiscated all his goods, and exiled him to Treviso. Foscari again tried to resign but was forced to remain in office.

By 1447 Jacopo was sick in body and mind. The Doge appealed to the Council of Ten to allow his son to return home. The Council agreed, because it was necessary to have a doge "whose mind is free and serene, able to serve the republic." Jacopo did not remain at home for long; in 1450 the Loredan family struck again.

That year Ermolao Donà was murdered. Jacopo was accused of the crime and tortured. Although nothing was proved, and it seemed likely that he was innocent, he was exiled to Crete. Even there he was carefully watched.

In 1456 he was suspected of plotting revenge with foreign help, and the Council of Ten had him brought back to Venice for trial.

It was clear that Jacopo was no threat to the republic, but that made no difference to the Council. He was tortured, found guilty, and again sentenced to exile in Crete, this time in prison. Before returning to Crete, he was allowed to see his father, who was now eighty-four years old. He begged the Doge to help him, to speak to the Council of Ten. "Jacopo," replied the old man, "go and obey your country's commands, and seek no more." But when Jacopo had gone, the Doge threw himself upon a chair, weeping and crying out. Within a few months he received word from Crete that his last son had died.

His enemies decided that this was the time to complete their victory. They said the Doge was too old. He was crushed by grief over his son and could no longer attend to business. Therefore, for the good of the republic, he must go. Foscari turned on them the argument that had been used against him in the past—he was forbidden by law from resigning without the agreement of the Greater Council. The Ten decided to disregard the law. They ordered him to resign and leave the palace within eight days. If he did, he would be given a good salary and a doge's burial when he died. If he still refused, he would be driven out and all his goods confiscated.

Foscari was forced to give in. The ring of the doge was taken from his finger and broken, the cap of the doge was taken from his head. He left the Palace wearing his old scarlet robe, bent and leaning on a staff. A week later he died of a burst blood vessel, just as the bells rang out to signal the election of a new doge. The people grumbled at the way the old man had been pushed out of office, and his enemies were a little ashamed that they had not waited another week for him to be removed by death. Now they gave him a splendid funeral, buried him in the church of the Frari, and honored him with a monument.

So ended the long reign of Francesco Foscari, one of the most important in the history of Venice. The Council of Ten had made certain that no one prince or family could win the rule of the city. Before 1457 seven doges had been assassinated, nine had been blinded and exiled, twelve had resigned, one had been sentenced to death and beheaded, two had been turned out of office. After 1457 Venice no longer feared the doge, and there was peace within the republic.

And it was under Foscari that Venice continued its policy of fighting land wars. No more did the city look only to the sea for its wealth; it was a land power as well as a sea power. There were years of danger, when Venice was forced to fight single-handed against the Turks. There were the even darker days when all the princes of Italy combined with other European powers against Venice in the League of Cambrai. Their aim was to ruin Venice—but Venice was not ruined. Its lands stretched from Lake Como in the west to Trieste in the east, from the high Alpine valleys in the north to Ferrara in the south. It ruled these rich territories wisely and well. They added enormously to Venetian wealth, in spite of the cost of the wars that had been fought to capture them.

The nobles found that it was far easier to get riches from the mainland than from the trade with the East. The Turks had taken Constantinople and trade with the East was more difficult than it had been in the time of the Greek emperors. Besides, trade with far places had always been something of a gamble. Many precious cargoes had been lost to pirates or swallowed by the stormy sea. But money invested in farms on the mainland brought in large, steady profits. The captured

A fresco from the Barbaro's sixty-six room villa

towns also offered other ways of making money—in real estate, banking, insurance, and partnerships in trade and industry.

The land itself, as well as the profits, attracted the Venetians. For centuries the wealthy families had built villas, or country houses, on the islands of Giudecca and Murano. In the landscaped gardens they had escaped the summer heat and stink of Venice. But tenements and warehouses were creeping along the Giudecca, while the buildings of the glass works were spreading over the Murano. The Venetian aristocrats took to the hills of Cadore or the gently sloping valley of the Brenta. There the architect Andrea Palladio built for them the most beautiful villas in the Western world. He used a style that would later, in the eighteenth century, be followed by architects in England and even in America.

The aristocrats enjoyed being landed gentlemen so much that they took less and less interest in being merchants. Although Venice

127

held its possessions in a tight grip, it no longer had the spirit of adventure. No Venetian ships went to explore America; no Venetian merchants searched for gold in tropical Africa. When Bartholomew Diaz sailed around the Cape of Good Hope in 1488, it meant the end of Venice's monopoly of trade with the East. Diaz had opened a new way to the Indies, and it would be the Portuguese, the Dutch, and the English who would take advantage of it.

During the great years of the Renaissance in Venice, from 1450 to 1570, the city was already losing its position as a leader in trade. It happened slowly, very slowly. The hard-headed merchants could still pile up profits; the government was still all-powerful. Yet Venice was changing from a city of commerce to a city of carnival, from a city of trade and merchants to a city of pleasure and pleasure-seekers. Venetians realized that Venice had lost the future, but they could still enjoy the glorious present. They turned to the new delights in painting, music, architecture, and literature that the Renaissance produced. They could well afford the cost, and the city had more than enough craftsmen to supply them with what they wanted. The result was that nowhere in Italy was there such an abundance of artistic luxuries—objects of gold and silver, armor, jewelry, bronzes, glass, lace.

Unlike other cities, Venice was quick to welcome the new craft of printing. By 1500 it had more than two hundred printing presses. Foremost of the printers was Aldus Manutius, who settled in Venice in 1490. He was determined to publish as many as possible of the Greek classics, so that they could be read by all. Surrounding himself with Greek scholars, Aldus worked day and night. Visitors to his office were warned by a notice on the door: "Whoever you are, Aldus begs you once and for all to state briefly what you want, and then leave quickly, unless you have come,

like Hercules, to support the weary Atlas on your shoulders, for that is what you will do when you enter this workshop." Aldus' books were moderately priced, well printed, and easy to read. Known as the Aldine Classics, they were famous throughout Europe.

But it was painting that most truly expressed the spirit of Venice during the Renaissance. The Signory had always believed in using art for propaganda. They were willing to pay high prices for huge frescoes in the Doge's Palace that depicted the heroic deeds of the republic or the noble acts of its great men. And when it came to a pageant, their hard fists opened willingly. Almost anything would do as an excuse for parading the might and splendor of the republic—saints' days, anniversaries of military victories, the signing of treaties, visits of kings or princes. Dressed in gorgeous costumes, senators and churchmen wound their way through the Piazza, or in and out of the Doge's Palace. Pageants were a way of teaching the people that the heads of the government were great and powerful. The Signory believed that the lesson could not be taught too often—and they hired outstanding artists to capture the pageants in paint and show the glories of the republic on the walls of the Doge's Palace.

Guilds and rich nobles followed the example of the Signory. They hired painters to decorate the walls of charity schools and hospitals, of churches and monasteries. The pictures showed scenes from the lives of the city's favorite saints, often painted against a background of Venice itself. There was so much demand for art that painting had to be done as a family affair. Every great Venetian painter was the director of a studio of painters in which brothers, wives, sons, daughters, assistants, and apprentices all worked together. These studios or workshops—they could even be called factories—produced hundreds of pictures. Every church, every monastery swarmed with masterpieces, and the city seemed almost overflowing with art.

One of the first artists to master the new technique of oil painting was Antonello da Messina. He learned it from the Flemish painters, and the Venetian painters in turn learned it from him. When he died they gave him a magnificent funeral, honoring him "not only for his pictures, which were distinguished by singular skill and beauty, but because . . . through mixing colors with oil, he first brought splendor and permanence to Italian painting." The most noted of the Venetian painters were the Bellini brothers and Giorgione, Titian, and Tintoretto. Some of their paintings were destroyed. The damp sea air ate away the frescoes on the palace walls, and the vast murals of Venetian history in the Doge's Palace were destroyed by fire. Nevertheless, an abundance of paintings remained as one of the great monuments of Western art. Other cities had nobler paintings, statues, and buildings, but the art of Venice had a quality of its own—a warmth, a glow, that came from the city's love of the world and the things of the world. Nowhere did the Renaissance last as late as it did in Venice, and nowhere was it more thoroughly a part of the everyday life of a city and its people.

The Venetians' delight in music is shown in this detail from a painting by Veronese.

THE GLORIES
OF VENETIAN
ART

Trade with the East gave Venetians a knowledge of the arts of the East—and from this came their love of rich colors. Early Venetian paintings were encrusted with gold, in imitation of Byzantine icons such as the image of the Archangel Michael (opposite), which was stolen from the Greeks in 1204 and deposited in Venice. Later painters never lost their love for color. From the East, too, came Venice's knowledge of certain crafts, particularly glassmaking. It was not true that the Venetian glassmakers turned out goblets that shattered on contact with poison. But their work was so amazingly skillful and delicate, as shown by the enameled goblet at left, that it did indeed seem magical.

Venetian painters were quick to take advantage of the great demand for portraits, and one of the busiest of them all was Titian. Giorgio Vasari, the Renaissance biographer of artists, said that there was "hardly a noble of high rank, scarcely a prince or a lady of great name whose portrait has not been painted by Titian." Except for the way in which he painted their gorgeous clothes, Titian did not flatter his sitters, as is shown in the picture of the bearded nobleman below.

Titian lived a long life, and continued working almost until the day of his death. He painted the unknown woman and the young Ranuccio Farnese at left. Young Man in a Red Cap (above) is thought to have been painted by either Vittore Carpaccio or Lorenzo Lotto. Apparently he did not possess luxurious clothing, which indicates that he was of lower rank than the persons portrayed by Titian.

In 828, when Venetian merchants stole the body of Saint Mark from its sarcophagus at Alexandria, it was said that the saint himself helped them by stirring up a storm. Years later, in the sixteenth century, Tintoretto painted the scene (left) for one of Venice's charitable societies. He also decorated the guildhall of another charitable society, which promised him an annual payment of a hundred ducats in exchange for three pictures a year. Across the forty-foot wall of one room he painted a vast Crucifixion. Above is a detail from it, showing Nicodemus, left, and the young Apostle John.

135

THE RENAISSANCE MAN

During the Renaissance, Venice, Rome, Milan, and Florence were being rebuilt. They were cities in construction, littered with scaffolding. Wherever people gathered—in the villas, the taverns, the piazzas, the gardens —they discussed the new cathedrals and palaces. The statues that adorn the Piazza della Signoria at Florence had not yet had time to weather; they were still a raw, gleaming white. At Venice the shops that spoiled the beauty of the Piazza San Marco were torn down. In Milan, crowds gathered to stare admiringly at the new citadel of the Sforza. The same story could be told of Mantua, of Parma, of Perugia, of Viterbo, of Genoa—in fact, of all the towns of Italy. New buildings and statues were rising, changing the look of familiar scenes, making the past seem far away.

In the churches and monasteries, scarcely a

By presenting the classical ideal of man with a new force and power, Michelangelo made his statue of David a symbol of Renaissance man.

year passed without a new masterpiece being painted on the walls. Today the surfaces of the paintings are dark with age, the colors faded. It is difficult to imagine how fresh and strange and original these pictures looked to those who first saw them. The same is true of the statues and bronzes. Printed books, too, were a novelty then. What a miracle it must have seemed to scholars to have their own copies of Virgil or Cicero, or to see their own writings stacked by the hundreds in printers' shops

The world was expanding. Stories from Spain and Portugal, tales from Genoese sea captains, told of wondrous continents that had never before been dreamed of. The discoveries of Columbus, of the Cabots, of the Portuguese in the Eastern Seas, showed that the stories were more than pretty fables. They were one more proof that this age was original and new, and that the immediate past was dead. People began to think of themselves in a new way. They felt free—free to think as they pleased, free to act as they pleased, free to live any kind of life they wished.

137

"Men are themselves the source of their own fortune and misfortune," said one Renaissance writer. Another said that to man "it is granted to have whatever he chooses, to be whatever he wills." If it was possible to reach greatness, it was also possible to suffer failure. A man might benefit by the wisdom of the past, or learn something from philosophy and religion. But in the end, what happened to him depended upon himself—on his nature and on his luck, which was of course controlled by God in some mysterious manner.

A good part of this belief came about because of the changing society, in which merchants gambled for profits on their own judgment and cleverness. At the same time, men were still priests, monks, scholars, soldiers, aristocrats, and merchants. Each group had a certain place in society, with rules, regulations, and beliefs centuries old. Sometimes the old beliefs conflicted with the new, and the result was that both were changed. More often than not, however, it was the new beliefs that won out, and this changed customs, influenced the arts, and even had an effect on politics.

Even more important, there were men whose very lives seemed shaped by the new beliefs. Among them was Pietro Aretino, who was an author, a wit, and a kind of literary blackmailer. "I am a free man," Aretino wrote. "I do not need to copy Petrarch or Boccaccio. My own genius is enough. Let others worry themselves about style and so cease to be themselves. Without a master, without a model, without a guide, without artifice, I go to work and earn my living, my well-being, and my fame. What do I need more? With a goose quill and a few sheets of paper I mock the universe."

Aretino was born in 1492, the son of a poor shoemaker. He passed himself off as the son of

A portrait of Pietro Aretino, one of the many painted by his friend and drinking-companion Titian.

a nobleman until someone who knew better gave him away. Then he boasted of the truth as loudly as he had told the lie. He received no serious education. He left home when he was twelve years old, and worked in Perugia as a painter's apprentice. Already he had begun to scribble verses. By 1516 he was in Rome, where he was attached to the household of the great Roman banker Agostino Chigi. Aretino's enemies later said that he had been a servant and was dismissed for stealing the silver. Aretino claimed that Chigi was his patron, not his master. At any rate, Chigi's household gave him a lifelong taste for luxury and good living. And it was while he was in Chigi's household that he began writing the amusing, satirical verses that would make him famous throughout Italy.

Rome was the perfect place for someone of Aretino's abilities. At the corner of the Piazza Navona stood a worn antique statue which was used as a bulletin board. Anyone who wanted to make fun of the leading citizens of Rome would write out his satire on a sheet of paper, which would then be stuck to the statue. Romans called the statue Pasquino, naming it after a sharp-tongued schoolmaster, and the satires became known as pasquinades. Most of them were fairly mild—but not Aretino's. His big chance came when the cardinals met to elect a new pope after the death of Pope Leo X. Aretino wrote a series of verses poking fun at the cardinals and the candidates. He raked up every shameful and dishonest thing they or their families had ever done. He showed them no mercy. What he did not know, he imagined—and he had a rich imagination.

All Rome rocked with laughter. The verses were printed and sold as handbills. Princes wrote to their ambassadors in Rome, asking for copies. No one believed Aretino would go unpunished, but he did. However, when Adrian VI was elected pope, Aretino wisely went off to Mantua. There he was welcomed by the Gonzaga family. After Clement VII, a Medici, became pope, he was called back to Rome to amuse the papal court. His reputation for wit and daring rose even higher, but again Rome became too dangerous for him, and off he went to join the famous condottiere Giovanni delle Bande Nere. In that great captain he saw a man like himself, a man who lived life in his own way. Giovanni was mortally wounded in battle, and Aretino described his death in one of the most remarkable letters he ever wrote. In simple and noble language, he told of the last hours of a heroic man accepting death, making his own terms with God as he had with man.

More bitter than ever, Aretino brought out a mock almanac. He made fun of men and their affairs by pretending to predict what would happen in the coming year of 1527. No one who displeased him escaped his sharp pen. He attacked princes and even the Pope himself. The almanac was an enormous success, and he began to get rich. Part of his riches came from the things he wrote; whatever he put down on paper sold well. The other part of his riches came from the things he did not write, from a kind of blackmail. Afraid of being laughed at, princes sent him gifts so that he would flatter them in print or avoid mentioning them altogether. Often he threatened to attack them unless he was paid. They almost always paid, and he could boast that "my pen has drawn more than 25,000 gold crowns from the entrails of various princes." In spite of this, he was liked as well as feared. Even the Pope finally forgave him and pampered him.

Wealthy and famous, he settled down in Venice. He lived like a prince in a palace on the Grand Canal, which he called the finest highway in the world. He was a good judge of painting and became a great friend of Titian's. The two drank together, feasted together, and carried on long discussions of art and life. Titian twice painted his portrait, and in return Aretino helped him get commissions. Aretino's house was always open, not only to his friends, but to the poor and unfortunate. He shared his wealth freely, and almost ruined himself with his generosity every Christmas. When he was an old man he could no longer afford to pay the rent on his palace, and he was forced to move away from the Grand Canal. He died at the age of sixty-four, struck down by apoplexy after he had laughed too hard at a joke.

Another Renaissance man who lived in the same fashion as Aretino was Benvenuto Cellini, the master craftsman. According to Cellini himself, Pope Paul III said of him, "Men like Benvenuto, unique in their profession, stand above the law." Pope Paul may or may not have said it, but there is no doubt that Cellini believed it. Besides being a gold-smith and sculptor, he was an adventurer, a hot-tempered brawler, and a murderer. And yet as an artist he was hardworking and tremendously talented. His services were in demand by popes and princes alike. Pope Clement VII called him "the greatest artist in his craft who was ever born." True, this again was according to Cellini himself. But a letter from Michelangelo to Cellini still exists, and in it Michelangelo wrote: "I have known you all these years as the greatest goldsmith of whom the world has ever heard."

Most of Cellini's works were small, and few have survived. But he also left behind a book, his *Autobiography*. A boastful, bragging account of his adventures in love, his quarrels, his bargaining with patrons, his struggles to master his art, it remains a clear picture of the life of the craftsman during the Renaissance.

Both Aretino and Cellini followed their own natures and lived by their own rules. They seemed to represent the man of the Renaissance, in contrast to the man of the Middle Ages, who was hemmed in by custom and rules made by others. But it must be remembered that Aretino was a writer and Cellini an artist. Perhaps the prince and the captain of war more truly represented the man of the Renaissance. In war and politics, all that mattered was to survive, to succeed, to kill before being killed. For a prince to seize and hold power, he had to live without principles of any kind. At least, that is what many people of the Renaissance believed. This belief was expressed most strongly by Niccolo Machiavelli in *The Prince*, a small book of advice to rulers on how to govern. Machiavelli took it for granted that men in general were selfish, cowardly, greedy, stupid, and easy to fool. The world of politics was a jungle, and a ruler had to use cruelty, cunning, and deceit to keep his power.

In later years, long after the Renaissance, Machiavelli's name itself came to mean treachery. And yet, curiously, Machiavelli himself was anything but treacherous. He was born a Florentine, of a family that had been active in politics for more than two centuries. He once wrote that politics was the passion of his life, that he could think and talk of nothing else, and it is likely that this began to be true when he was still young.

In 1498, when he had just turned twenty-nine, he was appointed second chancellor of the Florentine republic. Soon after, he was also made secretary to an important government committee, the Ten of Liberty and Peace. Actually, the committee was more concerned with war than with peace. Foreign armies were tramping back and forth across Italy, and Machiavelli took part in the diplomatic bargaining that always accompanied war during the Renaissance. He was sent on a number of diplomatic missions in Italy, Germany, and France. On these missions he had the chance to observe Cesare Borgia, and that ferocious prince became his hero.

Machiavelli had Cesare Borgia in mind when he wrote: "Everybody knows how laudable it is in a prince to keep his faith and to be an honest man and not a trickster. Nevertheless, the experience of our times shows that the princes who have done great things are the ones who have taken little account of their promises and who have known how to addle the brains of men with craft. In the end they have conquered those who put their reliance on good faith.

"You must realize then that there are two ways to fight. In one kind the laws are used, in the other, force. The first is suitable to man, the second to animals. But because the first often falls short, one has to turn to the second. Hence a prince must know perfectly how to act like a beast and like a man. . . .

"Since, then, it is necessary for a prince to understand how to make good use of the conduct of the animals, he should select among them the fox and the lion, because the lion cannot protect himself from traps, and the fox cannot protect himself from the wolves. So the prince needs to be a fox that he may know how to deal with traps, and a lion that he may frighten the wolves. Those who act like the lion alone do not understand their business. A prudent ruler, therefore, cannot and should not observe faith when such observance is to his disadvantage and the causes that made him give his promise have vanished. If men were all good, this advice would not be good, but since men are wicked and do not keep their promises to you, you likewise do not have to keep yours to them. Lawful reasons to excuse his failure to keep them will never be lacking to a prince. . . . the prince who has best known how to act as a fox has come out best. But one who has this capacity must understand how to keep it covered and be a pretender and a dissembler. Men are so simple and so subject to present needs that he who deceives in this way will always find those who will let themselves be deceived."

In war or politics, then, men might act like animals. With the boldness of the lion or the cunning of the fox, they might slash and claw their way to power. But life was more than wealth and power and fame, more than blood and violence and outwitting the enemy. Man was a social being as well as a political being, and needed to know how to act in human society. The difficulty was that society was changing. Ancestry was no longer of the greatest importance, as it had been during the Middle Ages. Few of the Renaissance rulers could boast of their ancestors. The Sforza rose from peasants to princes within three generations. Even the Medici had not started as aristocrats. Tough soldiers and rough merchants were becoming wealthy everywhere in Italy, and they wanted to learn manners that would match the luxury they could now afford. They wanted to be gentlemen.

Some of what they had to learn was just a matter of simple behavior. They studied the guide to behavior written between 1551 and 1555 by Giovanni della Casa. In it he said:

"To help you understand how to behave I must first teach you that your conduct should not be governed by your own fancy, but in consideration of the feelings of those whose company you keep. . . . when you have blown your nose, you should not open your handkerchief and inspect it, as though pearls or rubies had dropped out of your skull. Such

Humanist, architect, painter, writer on many subjects, Leon Battista Alberti was a typical Renaissance man.

In his life as well as in his writings, Baldassare Castiglione showed what a true gentleman should be.

behavior is nauseating and is more likely to lose us the affection of those who love us than to win us the favor of others. . . . It is not polite to scratch yourself when you are seated at table. You should also take care, as far as you can, not to spit at mealtimes, but if you must spit, do so in a decent manner. . . . We should also be careful not to gobble our food so greedily as to cause ourselves to get hiccups or commit some other unpleasantness . . . It is also bad manners to clean your teeth with your napkin, and still worse to do it with your finger, for such conduct is unsightly. It is wrong to rinse your mouth and spit out wine in public, and it is not a polite habit, when you rise from the table, to carry your toothpick either in your mouth, like a bird making its nest, or behind your ear. . . .

"It is also unmannerly to sprawl over the table or to fill both sides of your mouth so full with food that your cheeks are bloated. And you must do nothing to show that you have great relish in the food or the wine, for these are the customs of the tavern and the ale-house. . . . I do not think it right to offer food from one's own plate to anyone else, unless the person who offers it is of much more exalted rank, in which case it would be a mark of honor for the other. If both are of the same rank, it is rather a presumption of superiority for one of them to offer his food to the other, and sometimes the tidbit might not be to his taste. . . . You should neither comb your hair nor wash your hands in the presence of others, because—except for washing the hands before going in to a meal—such things are done in the bedroom and not in public. . . . Again, you must not appear in public with your nightcap on your head or fasten your hose when other people are present. . . ."

Of course, being a gentleman meant more than knowing how to behave with reasonable politeness in public. Giovanni della Casa himself said that no man could be a gentleman without modesty, without being "very desirous of beautiful things, well-proportioned and comely." The humanist Vittorino da Feltre went even farther. Being a gentleman was not just a matter of correct conversation or well-chosen clothes. On the contrary, it was the whole being of man; indeed, the highest perfection a man could achieve was to be immediately recognized as a gentleman.

Vittorino believed the education of a gentleman should begin at an early age, and he set up a boarding school for children in Mantua. His aim was to form character as well as mind and body. His pupils studied Latin and mathematics, and practiced such sports as riding, dancing, and swordsmanship. They were given exercises so that they would learn quickness of eye, control of the muscles, and grace of movement. They were taught to be courageous and hardy, and to withstand pain and discomfort. Above all, they were taught an appreciation of art and literature. Vittorino's pupils included the poor as well as the rich, girls as well as boys. One of his pupils was Federigo da Montefeltro, who later summed up the accomplishment of his teacher. Vittorino, he said, had instructed him "in all human excellence."

Federigo himself proved to be a good example of "human excellence." Unlike Aretino and Cellini, he represented the gentle side of Renaissance man. He was far from the kind of ruler pictured by Machiavelli in *The Prince*. At the same time, he was a condottiere, and his business was making war for pay. His family ruled the little hill town of Urbino, which had poor soil and was far from any of the important trade routes. Since the town could not live by either farming or trade, the Montefeltro family sold its services and its army to one side or the other in most of the Italian wars. So, after his schooling with Vittorino, Federigo was trained to be a professional soldier.

In 1444 he became the Duke of Urbino. He fought for Florence, Milan, Naples, and Rome, rarely losing a battle. For a Renaissance warrior, Federigo was unusual. He was a man of honor who never deserted his allies or broke his word. Never cruel or brutal, he was generous with his foes. He was as good a ruler as he was a general. He was popular with his people and had no fear of being assassinated. Vespasiano da Bisticci wrote of him that "when he rode out he met none who did not salute him and ask how he did. He went about with few attendants; none of them armed . . . He would often go afoot through his lands, entering now one shop and now another, and asking the workmen what their calling was, and whether they were in need of aught. So kind was he, that they all loved him as children love their parents. The country he ruled was a wondrous sight."

Under Federigo, Urbino became one of the great cultural centers of Europe. To Urbino came sculptors from Milan and Florence, architects from Siena and Dalmatia, painters from Spain and tapestry workers from Flanders. Raphael was born there. Within its walls worked Paolo Uccello, Piero della Francesca, and Melozzo da Forli. A list of Federigo's palace officers shows that five hundred persons were attached to the court. Besides knights and men-at-arms, there were two hundred servants, five architects and engineers, four teachers, an astrologer, five "readers aloud at meals," four men who transcribed manuscripts, two organists, the keeper of the bloodhounds, and a man who tended the giraffe, which was then called a camelopard.

Federigo's greatest joy was books. Vespasiano, who helped him build up his library, wrote, "He spared neither cost nor labor, and when he knew of a fine book, whether in Italy or not, he would send for it . . . and he always employed, in Urbino, in Florence, and in other places, thirty or forty scribes in his service. . . ." In addition to works on philosophy, history, and medicine in Greek and Latin, "there were to be seen Hebrew books, all that could be found in that language, beginning with the Bible, and all those who have commented upon it, Rabbi Moses and other commentators. Not only are those Hebrew books the Holy Scriptures, but also

on medicine, on philosophy, and in all branches, all that could be acquired in that tongue."

Federigo "delighted greatly in music, understanding vocal and instrumental alike, and maintained a fine choir with skilled musicians and many singing boys. He had every sort of instrument in his palace and delighted in their sound, also the most skillful players. He preferred delicate to loud instruments, caring little for trombones and the like."

Architecture was another of Federigo's delights. Vespasiano said that "no one of his age, high or low, knew it so thoroughly. We may see, in the buildings he constructed, the grand style and the due measurement and proportion, especially in his palace, which has no superior amongst the buildings of the time, none so well considered, or so full of fine things. Though he had his architects about him, he always first realized the design and then explained the proportions and all else; indeed to hear him discourse thereanent, it would seem that his chief talent lay in this art; so well he knew how to expound and carry out its principles."

Federigo tried to learn some new thing every day. He studied history and philosophy, and was skillful in arithmetic and geometry. Nor did he neglect religion. He knew the Scriptures well, went to Mass daily, and often discussed religion with the abbot or mother superior of one of the monasteries he supported. He lived simply, "eating plain food and no sweetmeats," and his court followed his example. There was no "romping or wrangling, but everyone spoke with becoming modesty."

Federigo da Montefeltro, who made the little town of Urbino a great center of culture.

144

An illustration from a Renaissance spelling primer

Federigo died in 1482, and his son Guidobaldo became Duke of Urbino. Guidobaldo, too, was a condottiere, and among those who joined his army was Baldassare Castiglione, a soldier who later became a diplomat. Castiglione came to the palace at Urbino to recover from a broken ankle and stayed for eleven years, sometimes going on diplomatic missions. He was charmed by the court, where people of all kinds—poets, priests, philosophers, condottieri, scholars, artists, singers, musicians—were welcome. He was even more charmed by Elisabetta, Guidobaldo's gentle and intelligent wife.

Guidobaldo and Elisabetta were equally charmed by Castiglione, and the three became close friends. They spent their evenings with other members of the court and whatever noted visitors had come to Urbino. They sang, they danced, they played games, they listened to instrumental music or watched theatricals. Above all, they carried on conversations. They spoke of many things—of love, of beauty, of the arts, of philosophy, of the nature of man.

Castiglione wrote a book titled *The Courtier*. In the form of the conversations that took place at Urbino, it was a discussion of what made a man a gentleman. Castiglione believed that a gentleman should be of noble birth, though this was not absolutely necessary. A gentleman had to be skilled in the art of war. He had to be strong and courageous, and therefore he had to learn certain sports— horsemanship, fencing, and wrestling. "He should also know," wrote Castiglione, "how to swim, jump, run, throw stones; for, besides their usefulness in war, it is frequently necessary to show one's prowess in such things, whereby a good name is to be won, especially with the crowd (with whom one must reckon after all). Another noble exercise and most suitable for a man at court is the game of tennis which shows off the disposition of body, the quickness and litheness of every member, and all the qualities that are brought out by almost every other exercise."

Of course, a gentleman had to have learning. Castiglione advised that he should be "conversant not only with the Latin language, but with Greek as well, because of the abundance and variety of things that are so divinely written therein. Let him be versed in the poets, as well as in the orators and historians, and let him be practiced also in writing verse and prose . . . for, besides the personal satisfaction he will take in this, in this way he will never want for pleasant entertainment with the ladies, who are usually fond of such things." And he should appreciate and know something of the arts, of painting and sculpture and music and architecture.

Whatever he did, a gentleman should do gracefully, "so as to conceal all art and make whatever is done and said appear to be without effort and without almost any thought about it." He should be modest, never going too far in showing his skill. For example, when dancing in a place full of people, "he should maintain a certain dignity, though tempered with a fine and airy grace of movement; and even though he may feel himself to be most agile and a master of time and measure, let him not attempt those quick movements of foot and those double steps which . . . little befit a gentleman."

In some things he should not even try to develop great skill. The game of chess, wrote Castiglione, "is certainly a pleasing and ingenious amusement . . . but it seems to me to have one defect, which is that it is possible to have too much knowledge of it, so that whoever would excel in the game must give a great deal of time to it, as I believe, and as much study as if he would learn some noble science or perform well anything of importance; and yet in the end, for all his pains, he only knows how to play a game. Thus, I think a very unusual thing happens in this, namely, that mediocrity is more to be praised than excellence."

Castiglione's book was published in 1528. By 1538 it had been translated into French, by 1561 into English. It set the pattern for gentlemanly conduct not only for its own time but for modern times as well. Baldassare Castiglione, Vittorino da Feltre, and Federigo da Montefeltro, all Renaissance men, established standards of behavior and education for years to come.

This woodcut is from a book on the game of chess published in Florence in 1493.

I E
FA
ni
St
au
lu
ria
qu
la

perio comminuitur · Quid
nomini gloriam querimus
dulcedinem aliquam haur

PEOPLE OF THE RENAISSANCE

The Renaissance gave new importance to men and women as individuals, and what they could accomplish. People tried to widen their knowledge and develop abilities in many fields. Doctors were interested in humanism as well as medicine; artists studied the sciences; monks created works of art; aristocrats became skilled musicians.

Typical of the Renaissance was the career of Pope Pius II, whose portrait at left is from a manuscript of one of his writings. He was born Aeneas Silvius Piccolomini, in 1405. As a young man, the life he led was far from religious. At the same time, he loved learning. "A miser is never satisfied with his money," he said, "nor a wise man with his knowledge." He was a scholar and a diplomat, and his missions took him all over Europe. He wrote a novel, a play, poetry, essays, travel sketches, and histories.

Not until he was past the age of forty did he become a priest. He rose rapidly, and within ten years he was a cardinal; within twelve, he was elected pope. He lived simply, carried out his duties well and faithfully, and died in 1464 while trying to lead a Crusade against the Turks.

This wood and stucco bust of an unknown woman (above), made by an artist who is also unknown, shows the kind of elegant beauty that was admired in Florence.

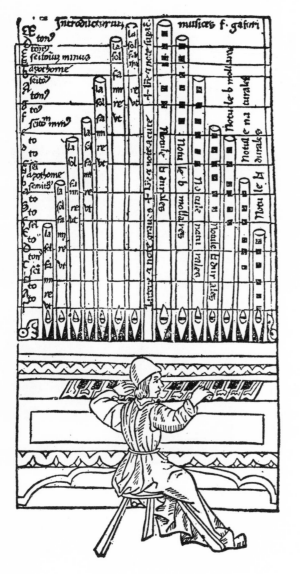

During the Renaissance, music was heard not only in the churches but in homes, on the streets, and in the courts of princes. It was played and sung in pageants, in festivals, in plays. While France, rather than Italy, led the way in the technical development of music, Italy had many outstanding performers. And Franchino Gafori, who taught at the famous music school in Milan, wrote several books that revolutionized the rules of composition and harmony. Woodcuts from his books show him (above) teaching a class in harmony and (left) demonstrating the hexachord system at the organ.

Fra Luca Pacioli's interest in mathematics began when he was a student of Alberti and Piero della Francesca. He was an author, a teacher, a friend of Leonardo da Vinci's, and became the head of his monastery. Of his many books on mathematics, the most outstanding was a huge volume published in 1494, Everything about Arithmetic, Geometry, and Proportion. *But his greatest fame came from his explanation of double-entry bookkeeping, which was given in the same book. This system of bookkeeping was of great importance to Italy's merchants and won Pacioli the title of "Father of Bookkeeping." In the painting above he is shown with a student, thought to be Guidobaldi, the young Duke of Urbino.*

In spite of their interest in scientific thought, the people of the Renaissance had a deep belief in astrology. Throughout Italy astrologists busily prepared horoscopes, advising rich and poor upon the most favorable time for everything from declaring war to planting trees. There were few learned men who did not believe in the power of the stars to influence human actions and natural events. In the painting above, the god Jupiter is depicted with two signs of the zodiac. At left is a detail from the astrological tables of G. Bianchini, which shows him presenting a copy to Emperor Frederick III.

Girolamo Fracastoro (right), a wealthy and brilliant physician, was one of the doctors who led Renaissance medicine away from the superstitions and miracle cures of the Middle Ages. The first doctor to recognize typhus, he became famous for his studies of contagious infections. During the Renaissance there were many advances in medicine. Leprosy was controlled by quarantine, laws were passed against quacks, and the number of hospitals multiplied. In the picture below, from a fifteenth-century manuscript, doctors are caring for hospitalized patients.

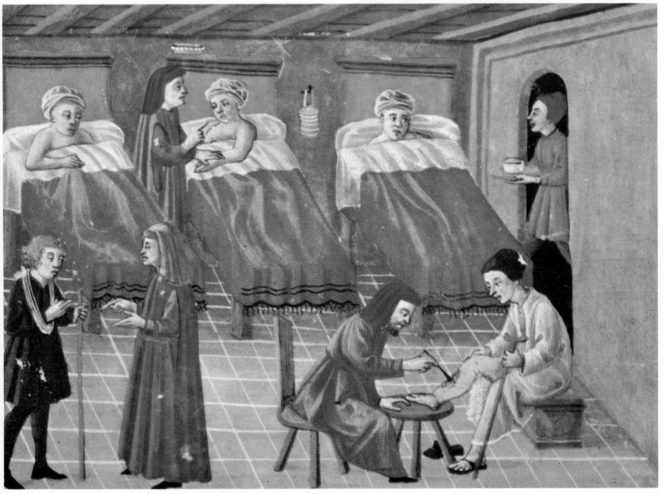

Within the monasteries of Italy were men of the highest talent, such as Fra Angelico, Fra Filippo Lippi, Fra Luca Pacioli, and Fra Bartolommeo. Besides the works of art produced by monks themselves, priors commissioned some of the masterpieces of the Renaissance. The monasteries also sponsored schools, hospitals, and charitable institutions. But it was a worldly age, and there were many scandals. Filippo Lippi, an artist and a monk, eloped with the young nun who was the model for the Virgin in the Madonna and Child (above). At left is the artist's portrait, in a detail from his tomb.

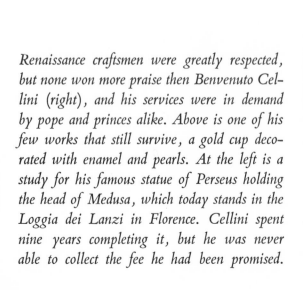

Renaissance craftsmen were greatly respected, but none won more praise then Benvenuto Cellini (right), and his services were in demand by pope and princes alike. Above is one of his few works that still survive, a gold cup decorated with enamel and pearls. At the left is a study for his famous statue of Perseus holding the head of Medusa, which today stands in the Loggia dei Lanzi in Florence. Cellini spent nine years completing it, but he was never able to collect the fee he had been promised.

155

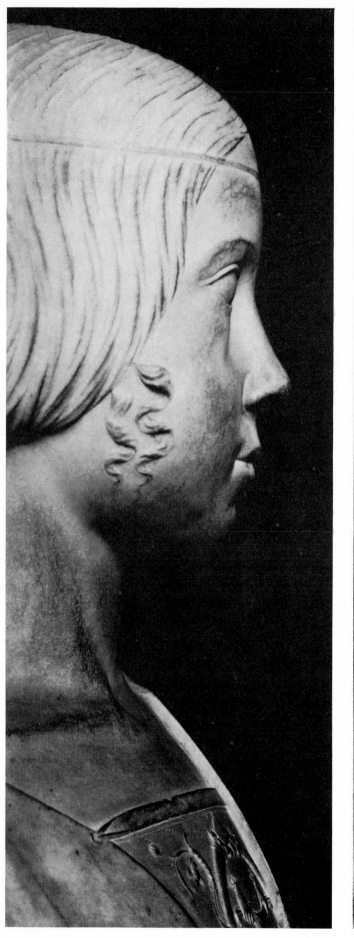

When Borso d'Este (above, left) died of malaria, his brother Ercole
became Duke of Ferrara. He married Leonora (below, right), a
beautiful Neopolitan princess. They had two daughters, Beatrice
(opposite, left) and Isabella (opposite, right), who were among
the most notable women of the Renaissance. The sisters were as
talented as they were beautiful, and were educated in literature
and the arts at the Este court in Ferrara. Beatrice, who was born
in 1475, was married to Lodovico Sforza (above, right) at the age
of sixteen. At her court in Milan she welcomed scholars, artists,
and poets, and she was a skillful diplomat. Isabella, who was
born in 1474, was also married at the age of sixteen. Her husband
was Francesco Gonzaga, the Marquis of Mantua (above, center).
She, too, made her court a center of art and learning, and was
skillful at diplomacy and politics. She ruled Mantua, and ruled
well, when Francesco was captured and imprisoned by the Venetians. She ruled again for a time after Francesco died and her nineteen-year-old son became Marquis. A poet called her la prima
donna del mondo—the first lady of the world. All of the remarkable Este family were talented. Ercole translated Latin plays
and staged them in the palace courtyard; Leonora was a harpist;
and an aunt of the sisters was famous for her writings in Latin.

THE SPREAD
OF THE
RENAISSANCE

In the autumn of 1511, the famous Dutch scholar Erasmus came to England for the third time. He was poor, he was frightened of the plague, and he was very lonely. For five weary years he stayed at Queen's College, Cambridge. When he could stand it no longer, off he went on his journeys again, to the Netherlands, to Switzerland, to Germany. Always he remembered his years of study in Italy, where the new learning of the Renaissance had filled him with hope. Even the sorrows and hardships of his personal life could not make him lose that hope. In 1517 he could still write, "Immortal God, what a world I see dawning! Why can I not grow young again?"

At the same time, Pietro Torrigiano, a gifted Florentine sculptor, was at work in

The château of Azay-le-Rideau, one of the first masterpieces of Renaissance art in France.

London. He was modeling tombs for Henry VII and his wife, the first Renaissance tombs of Northern Europe. For some time now, not only great events, such as the invasion of Italy by the French kings, but also the excitement of the new learning of the Renaissance, had been drawing men like Erasmus and Torrigiano into or out of Italy.

And there were others besides Erasmus who had a sense of wonder, of a new dawn, of a new world opening up before them. Henry VII made the Duke of Urbino's son a Knight of the Garter. This was one of the highest honors of the English court, and Castiglione came to England to receive it as the Duke's ambassador. Henry VII had so much respect for Italian scholarship that he asked Polydore Vergil to write a history of England. Indeed, Erasmus had come to England because of a band of humanists who had themselves studied Greek and philosophy in Padua, Florence, and Rome. This same band, which

159

Dürer painted this watercolor while in Italy.

included two men closely connected with the English royal family, was also responsible for bringing Pietro Torrigiano to London. The English humanists were deeply religious, and they used their humanistic studies as an aid to a more thorough understanding of Christianity. What was true of England was also true of the Netherlands, of Germany, and of Spain.

As the Renaissance spread beyond the Alps, it was checked in Italy. In 1495 Charles VIII invaded Naples, beginning thirty years of slaughter. Battle followed battle in the Lombard plain. Wealth was drained away, trade was ruined, taxes rose. Conditions were no longer favorable to art and learning. Furthermore, the riches of the New World, which had so recently been discovered, did not reach Italy. Instead, they poured into Spain, the Netherlands, France, and England. Wealth went west, and with wealth went art. Then, in 1517, Martin Luther rebelled against the Roman Catholic Church, setting off the Reformation. To defend itself against the

Reformation, the Papacy became stern. The luxurious and immoral days of the Borgia and the Medici were at an end, and Rome was not the city it had been.

By 1500 the art and thought of Italy were already deeply influencing Western Europe. The princes of the Western world wished to get the services of Italy's great painters and sculptors; the artists of the Western world were drawn to Italy to study the works of its artists. Only the Flemish painters had produced art that could stand comparison with the art of Italy. While they learned much from the Italians, the Italians learned as much from them.

With the French and German artists, the story was different. They were amazed by the books of engravings of Italian pictures that circulated in Europe after 1470. These engravings were no more than crude copies of paintings, but they filled the French and the Germans with a great curiosity.

Albrecht Dürer, while still a young apprentice at Nuremberg in Germany, studied the engravings of Pollaiuolo and Mantegna. They helped him get away from the harsh style of German art. Even so, the engravings were not enough for him. There was a mystery about them he could not solve. He believed the Italian painters had some secret method of successfully painting the human figure, a method which they kept well hidden. In 1494 he made his first trip to Italy, to see for himself "what had been hidden for a thousand years." The Renaissance was at its height, and young Dürer was swept along by it. He copied the paintings of Mantegna, studied mathematics, read Latin poetry. A generous Venetian painter taught him the mathematical secrets of drawing a perfectly proportioned human body. Dürer said that his new-found knowledge was more precious to him than a kingdom.

Velázquez' painting marks a victory over the Dutch in one of the wars waged by Spain against the Protestants.

Back in Nuremberg after a second trip to Italy, Dürer wrote books on painting and on human proportions. These, together with his own paintings, would revolutionize German art. In spite of his wife's nagging, he refused to leave his books and tend strictly to the trade of painting. His friends were humanists and scholars, rather than members of the painters' guild. Although Dürer's art was enriched by the ideas of the Renaissance, he never really mastered the Italian style of painting. He could not escape the German tradition into which he had been born. What happened to Dürer was very much like what happened to Germany itself. The Renaissance there was overcome by the Reformation, and a fanatical concern for religion pushed out the spirit of humanism.

For Dürer, the reformation of religion was an experience far deeper than his experience with art in Italy. And yet, without his experience in Italy, his work would have been less

161

noble. He was only one of the many artists who were influenced by the Italians. For the next four hundred years, scores of artists, both great and small, turned to Italy as the center of Western art. The work of El Greco, who had a style very much his own, showed the result of the years he spent in Venice. The way he drew, the way he edged his figures with glittering light, he learned from Tintoretto. From Titian he learned how to handle color. The two greatest French artists of the seventeenth century, Nicolas Poussin and Claude Lorraine, spent most of their working lives in Rome. Like El Greco, Poussin learned much from Titian. Again and again, artists of genius —Velàzquez, Rubens, Rembrandt, Goya, Renoir—used the same themes as the artists of the Renaissance, and sometimes even copied their pictures. Any artist who hoped to be great felt it necessary to make the long journey to Italy. Some, like Sir Joshua Reynolds, went in comfort, their expenses paid by rich patrons. Others, like Richard Wilson, went on foot, painting for their bread. Until the twentieth century, all Western and European artists worked in the traditions created by the Italian Renaissance.

The Renaissance spread to France in a rather special way. During their invasions of Italy, the French kings and their courtiers were delighted with what they saw. Noblemen with the armies of Charles VIII and Louis XII were entranced with the gardens, the clothes, the furnishings and decoration of houses and palaces, the general manner of life. Louis XII was so impressed by Leonardo da Vinci's fresco of the Last Supper that he wanted to cut it down from the wall and carry it back to France. His courtiers finally persuaded him not to do it. He was forced to satisfy his hunger for Italian art by arranging for a group of Italian craftsmen to work for him in France.

It was Francis I, the king who followed Louis XII, who really fell in love with Italy and Italian art. He was the first ruler outside Italy to begin a collection of paintings and sculpture by the great Italian masters. He did everything he could to get Michelangelo to live in France, but failed. He had to be content with buying a statue of Hercules. With Leonardo da Vinci and Benvenuto Cellini he was more successful. He managed to employ Leonardo by promising him seven thousand pieces of gold and "a palace of his own choice in the most beautiful region of France." Leonardo spent his last years at Amboise, close to Francis' hunting lodges at Blois and Chambord. To lure Cellini to Paris, Francis said to the goldsmith, "I will choke you with gold." Cellini received the same salary as Leonardo, but Francis gave Leonardo an additional sum of money when he bought the famous portrait of Mona Lisa.

Francis had a true appreciation of art and literature. He was as generous with praise as he was with money. When Cellini showed him the wax model of a golden saltcellar,

Francis I brought Renaissance art to France.

Francis said, "This is a hundred times more divine a thing than I had ever dreamed of." And when the piece was finished, Cellini reported later, "He uttered a loud cry of astonishment and could not satiate his eyes with gazing at it."

Along the valley of the river Loire, Francis and his nobles built splendid châteaux, or castles. They were designed by Italian architects and adorned in Renaissance style. Château life, too, was in Renaissance style, as it had been described by Castiglione. For Francis was not merely a collector. He wanted his court to outshine in literature and in manners, as well as in art, the most famous courts of Italy. He became the patron of anyone who might bring fame to France. In this he was aided by his remarkable sister, Marguerite of Navarre, one of the most outstanding women of the Renaissance. She was the patron of Rabelais, the greatest writer of the French Renaissance, and was herself the author of a book of stories and of religious poetry. Other women, too, played a large part in the French Renaissance. Francis imported Catherine de' Medici as a wife for his son, and she brought with her the tastes of the Medici as well as some of their cash. And then there were Mary Queen of Scots, the wife of Francis' grandson, and Diane de Poitiers. Artists looked to these women for support almost as much as to the kings themselves. Altogether, the French court could boast of people of great talent, especially in literature, who would have been a credit to any court in Italy. And, while they owed much to the Italian Renaissance, they had a style of their own, a style that was distinctly French.

In England, the Renaissance was an age of new men. The Wars of the Roses during the fifteenth century, when Englishman fought Englishman, tore English society apart. Later, Henry VIII broke with the Roman Catholic Church and took over the property of the monasteries. Within twenty years one-fifth of the country's land was up for sale, and wealthy merchants and lawyers bought as much of it as they could. Now they were landed gentlemen. They were the new men, and it was they, rather than the nobility, who were important in English society. One observer said that gentlemen "be made good cheap in England." It was not quite that easy. The times were dangerous, and a man needed a fierce spirit to rise in the world.

Still, as England's wealth increased, so did the numbers of gentlemen. They looked to Italy for guidance in politics, in diplomacy, in behavior. The English Renaissance reached its height during the reign of Queen Elizabeth I. Scholars studied Italian humanism, dandies dressed in the Italian fashion, playwrights lifted plots, characters, and sometimes whole plays from Italian authors. Even William Shakespeare, the greatest of Elizabethan writers, used numerous Italian scenes, characters, and tales in his plays.

The Italian Renaissance had an immense influence on art, literature, learning, and education in Western Europe. Even more important, however, was its influence on the

Shakespeare jeered at Englishmen who followed Italian fashions, but he used Italian tales in his plays.

Queen Elizabeth I visited Longleat, an English mansion designed and decorated in the Italian style.

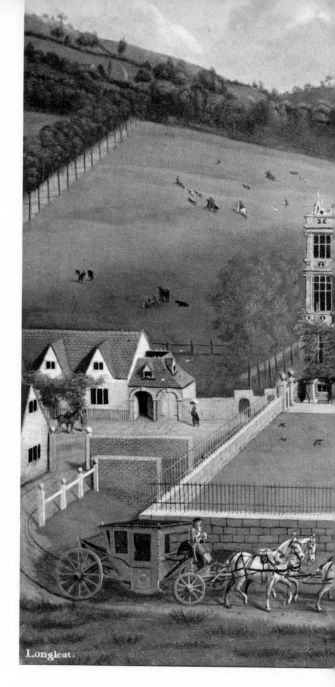

Longleat.

patterns of society. Except for Flanders, Italy had been the first country in Europe to grow really rich on trade. It had the first middle class which could challenge the power of the aristocracy. Merchants, bankers, and craftsmen found their first real safety in business life. This they knew; this they controlled. And so they organized their political and social life around their business activities, in the guilds. But their growing wealth and the needs of their professions forced them into contact with the aristocrats, who were still rich enough to have a privileged place in society. The result was a great change in customs, in manners, in education.

Once the merchants had gained wealth and power, they asked themselves, "How must we behave? What must we do to be gentlemen? What is a gentleman?" In their search for an answer, the Italians could do something that the Flemish could not. They could look back to the past, to the days of ancient Greece and Rome, when life had also been rich, aristocratic, and yet commercially minded.

By 1530 or so, Italian society had set up a new idea of what a gentleman should be. It was based on a combination of things learned from the days of Greece and Rome, from the more recent days of feudalism, from the middle class and the aristocracy, from country living and city living. This idea was important, because Western Europe was changing in the same way that Italy had changed between 1300 and 1450. In the sixteenth century, trade poured wealth into the cities of Cadiz, Lisbon, Bordeaux, Nantes, London, Antwerp, and Hamburg. There were new men not only in England, but in Spain, in Portugal, in France, in Flanders, in Germany.

These new men were numbered in the thousands, and they were uneasy about their position in society. They had to learn to be gentlemen—and so they took up the idea of the gentleman already established in Italy. They eagerly read books on behavior by the Italians della Casa and Castiglione. They followed the example of the Italians in clothes, in manners, in educating their children. From the North Cape of Norway to the Strait of Gibraltar, anyone who wanted to be a gentleman had to know a great deal of Latin and a

little Greek. A knowledge of the arts was as necessary as skill in riding a horse. But education in itself was not enough. As Castiglione had emphasized over and over again, a gentleman had to carry his knowledge lightly, with an air of nonchalance. By accepting this idea of the gentleman, the middle class was accepting the ideas of the aristocracy.

For years the spirit of the Renaissance was strong in Europe. It had bad effects as well as good ones. It encouraged snobbery and helped to keep men divided into classes. In education, it emphasized the development of a certain kind of character, rather than the development of particular abilities. But in return it gave much. It taught the new men of Europe how to live, and to use their wealth to support learning and art. And it taught that each man was an individual, with experiences unlike that of other men, and this idea led to some of the world's greatest art and literature. The spirit of the Renaissance bridged the centuries from the age of feudalism to modern times, and its influence can still be felt today.

165

PICTURE CREDITS

The source of each picture is listed below. The title or description appears after the page number, which is in boldface type, followed by the artist (where appropriate) and the location of the work. Where the location of a museum or library is obvious, the city has been omitted. Photographic credits appear in parentheses. Where two or more pictures appear on one page, they are separated by dashes.

The following abbreviations are used: Amb.—Biblioteca or Pinacoteca Ambrosiana, Milan; BEM—Biblioteca Estense, Modena; BLF—Biblioteca Laurenziana, Florence; BM—British Museum; BN—Bibliothèque Nationale, Paris; ENIT—Ente Nazionale Industrie Turistiche, Rome; LC—Library of Congress, Washington; MMA—Metropolitan Museum of Art, New York; MNF—Museo Nazionale, Florence; NGAW, Kress—National Gallery of Art, Washington, Kress Collection; NGAW, Widener—National Gallery of Art, Washington, Widener Collection; NGL—National Gallery, London; NYPL—New York Public Library; SGF—Soprintendenza alle Gallerie di Firenze

Half Title Mars. *De Sphaera.* Ms. A.X. 2.14, BEM (Aldo Martello Editore) *Title Page* "The Adimari Wedding." Anonymous. Gallerie dell' Accademia, Florence **5** Courtly scene. Boccaccio, *Decamerone*, Venice, 1525 **6** Cathedral, Orvieto (John Ross) **9** Venice. Ms. 264, Bodleian Library, Oxford **10-11** Map by David Greenspan **13** Horrors of tyranny. *De Sphaera.* Ms. A.X. 2.14, BEM (Aldo Martello Editore) **14** "Scene from the Life of San Bernardino." by the Master of Legend of San Bernardino. Pinacoteca Vanucci, Perugia **15** Colleoni by Verrocchio. Detail, Campo SS. Giovanni e Paolo, Venice (Anderson) **17** Gibbet by Pisanello. Detail of "St. George and the Princess of Trebizond." S. Anastasia, Verona **18-19** "The Return of Lodovico from Exile" by Mantegna. Camera degli Sposi, Castello di Corte, Mantua **20** "Return of Cardinal Francesco Gonzaga from Rome" by Mantegna. Camera degli Sposi, Castello di Corte, Mantua **21** Sigismondo Malatesta by Piero della Francesca. Detail of fresco. Tempio. Malatestiano. Rimini (Scala) **22** Old woman. Tuscan majolica. Fitzwilliam Museum, Cambridge **22-23** Bas-relief of craftsmen by Nanni di Banco. Orsanmichele, Florence (Alinari) **24** "Madonna and Child" by Piero della Francesca and assistants. Brera, Milan **25** "The Castelfranco Madonna" by Giorgione. Cathedral, Castelfranco Veneto (Conzett & Huber) **26** Drawing tools. Museum of the History of Science, Oxford **26-27** Ideal city attributed to Piero della Francesca. Palazzo Ducale, Urbino (Anderson) **28** S. Francesco, Arezzo (Gjon Mili) **29** Plaques on Campanile, Florence, by Giotto, Andrea Pisano, and others (All: Alinari) **30** "Pietà" by Giotto. Scrovegni Chapel, Padua (Scala) **31** "St. Jerome in his Study" by Antonello da Messina. NGL—Unloading wheat by Fra Angelico. Detail of "Scene from the Life of St. Nicholas of Bari" Pinacoteca Vaticana (Istituto Italiano d'Arti Grafiche, Bergamo) **32-33** "The Flagellation of Christ" by Piero della Francesca. Palazzo Ducale, Urbino (Scala) **33** Face by Leonardo da Vinci. Palazzo Reale, Turin (Anderson)—Head by Piero della Francesca, *De Prospettiva pingendi.* Amb.—Mosaic attributed to Uccello. Atrium, San Marco (Osvaldo Böhm)—Chalice by Uccello. Uffizi (SGF) **34** Presumed portrait of Cecilia Gallerani. "Lady with an Ermine" by Leonardo da Vinci. Museum Czartoryskich, Cracow (Kindler Verlag, Munich)—Leonello d'Este by Pisanello. NGAW, Kress **35** Giovanni di Pierfrancesco de' Medici by Botticelli. Collection of Sir Thomas Merton **36-37** "Diana and Actaeon" by Titian. Ellesmere Collection, National Gallery, Edinburgh (Larry Burrows, courtesy *Life*) **37** Drawing by Signorelli. Louvre (Giraudon) **38** "The Adoration of the Shepherds" by Giorgione. Detail. NGAW, Kress—"St. Jerome" attributed to Lazzaro Bastiani. Museum of Fine Arts, Boston **38-39** "St. Francis in Ecstasy" by Giovanni Bellini. The Frick Collection (Courtesy *Time*) **40** View from Boboli Gardens (Robert Descharnes) **42** Arms of Arte della Lana attributed to Luca della Robbia. Museo dell' Opera del Duomo (Alinari) **42-43** Facsimile of woodcut in Staatliche Museen, Berlin. Print Division, NYPL **44** Abundance. *Il Biadajolo.* Tempiano 3, BLF (ENIT) **45** Cosimo de' Medici. Detail of "Procession of the Magi" by Benozzo Gozzoli. Palazzo Medici-Riccardi (Scala) **47** Lorenzo de' Medici by Verrocchio. NGAW, Kress (William Sumits, courtesy *Life*) **48-49** "Tournament in the Piazza Santa Croce" by the Master of the Jarves *Cassone.* Jarves Collection, Yale University Art Gallery **50** "The Youthful David" by Andrea del Castagno. NGAW, Widener (Courtesy *Metropolitan Museum of Art Miniatures* and Book-of-the-Month Club) **51** Giuliano de' Medici by Botticelli, NGAW, Kress **52** Medal of Pico della Mirandola attributed to Niccolo Fiorentino. BN (Giraudon) **55** Savonarola by Fra Bartolommeo. Detail Museo San Marco **56** "Burning of Savonarola." Anonymous. Museo San Marco **58** "Judith and Holofernes" by Donatello. Piazza della Signoria (Alinari)—Cup. Museo degli Argenti (SGF) **59** "Allegory of the Divine Comedy" by Domenico di Michelino. Detail. Cathedral (Istituto Geografico de Agostini, Novara) **60** Self-portrait (Brogi) From second doors by Ghiberti. Baptistery **60-61** Second doors by Ghiberti. Baptistery (Anderson) **61** Sacrifice of Isaac (Anderson) and squirrel (Brogi). From second doors by Ghiberti. Baptistery **62** "St. Augustine" by Botticelli. Ognissanti **63** "Adoration of the Magi" by Fra Angelico and Fra Filippo Lippi. NGAW, Kress **64-65** "The Procession of the Magi" by Benozzo Gozzoli. Palazzo Medici-Riccardi (Fernand Bourges, courtesy *Life*) **66** Cathedral (Foto Paoletti) **69** Armor. MMA **71** Sebastian Muenster, *Cosmographia*, 1588. LC **72** Assassination. Lorenzo della Rota, *Lamento del Duca Galeazo*, Florence 1505 **74** Detail from Velins 724, BN **75** Detail from Velins 724, BN **76** Certosa of Pavia. Detail of "The Carthusians Following Christ" by Borgognone. Musei Civici, Pavia **77** Portals by Giovanni Antonio Amadeo. Certosa of Pavia (Alinari) **78** Massimiliano Sforza. Portrait Cod. 2167, Biblioteca Trivulziana **79** Massimiliano Sforza on horseback. Cod. 2167, Biblioteca Trivulziana **80** Self-portrait byLeonardo. Palazzo Reale, Turin (Alinari) **81** Vitruvian man. Gallerie dell' Accademia, Venice (Alinari) **82** All : Royal Collection, Windsor Castle. Copyright reserved. **83** Parachute *Codice Atlantico*, Amb.—Wing and leverage demonstration. Ms. B, Institut de France. Fascimile **84** Snorkel. Cod. Arundel, BM—Dredge. Ms. E, Institut de France (Giraudon)—Automotive wagon. *Codice Atlantico*, Amb.—Spiral staircase and two-decker city. Ms. B, Institut de France. Facsimile **85** *Lilium candidum* and bramble. Royal Collection, Windsor Castle. Copyright reserved—Crabs. Kölnisches Stadtmuseum, Cologne **86** Michelangelo, from his atelier. Louvre **87** Drawings of Hercules by Michelangelo. Royal Collection, Windsor Castle. Copyright reserved **88** "Pietà" by Michelangelo. St. Peter's (Anderson) BM **88-89** Model of a river god by Michelangelo. Galleria dell' Accademia, Florence **89** Nude athlete by Michelangelo. Detail of ceiling. Sistine Chapel, Vatican (Anderson) **90** "Rondanini Pietà" by Michelangelo. Castello Sforzesco, Milan (Arc. Fot. dei Civici Musei, Milan) **91** Sistine Chapel **92** Tempietto. S. Pietro in Montorio, Rome (Georgina Masson, courtesy Thames and Hudson) **94** Pius II by Paolo Romano. Appartamento Borgia, Vatican (Anderson)— Nicholas V, Sixtus IV, Clement VII. All BN **95** Alexander VI and Julius II. BN—Leo X. NGAW, Kress **96** The Forum (Dmitri Kessel) **97** "Apollo Belvedere." Musei Vaticani (Anderson) **98** Pope Sixtus IV in the Vatican Library. Florentine School. 16th century. Ospedale di Santo Spirito (courtesy Prof. Pietro De Angelis) **99** Sixtus IV and Platina by Melozzo da Forlì. Pinacoteca Vaticana (Scala) **100** "Paul III with Alessandro and Ottavio Farnese" by Titian. Galleria Nazionale, Naples **103** Julius II by Raphael. Detail of "Mass of Bolsena." Stanze, Vatican **104-105** "Sack of Rome" Probably by Pieter Brueghel the Elder. Collection of M. Destombes, Paris **106** "St. Lawrence Giving Alms" by Fra Angelico. Chapel of Nicholas V **107** "St. Jerome" by Leonardo da Vinci. Pinacoteca Vaticana (Eric Schaal, courtesy *Time*) **108** "School of Athens" by Raphael. Stanze (Archivio Fotografico, Mus. Vat.)—Grotesque by Giovanni da Udine. Logge (Archivio Fotografico, Mus. Vat.) **109** "Disputation on the Sacrament" by Raphael. Detail. Stanze (Scala) **110-111** "Punishment of Korah, Dathan, and Abiram" by Botticelli. Sistine Chapel **112-113** Ceiling of the Sistine Chapel by Michelangelo. Detail. Vatican (Anderson) **114** Piazza San Marco (G.E. Kidder Smith) **116-117** View of Venice by Jacapo de' Barbari. Facsimile. NYPL, Print Division **118-119** "Healing of the Demoniac" by Carpaccio. Gallerie dell' Accademia, (Foto Fiorentini) **120** The Doge's *Bucentaur.* Yale University Library, Rare Books (Loebel) **121** Lion's mouth. Museo Correr **122-123** "Corpus Christi Procession" by Gentile Bellini. Gallerie dell' Accademia, Venice (Eric Schaal, courtesy *Life*) **126** Villa Foscari, "La Malcontenta" (Giuseppi Fini) **127** Hunter by Veronese. Villa Barbaro at Maser (Alinari) **129** "Wedding at Cana" by Veronese. Louvre (Giraudon) **130** Goblet. Cleveland Museum of Art (Carter Jones, courtesy *Time*) **131** Icon. Tesoro di San Marco (Millet, *Connaissance des Arts*) **132** "Portrait of a Man" by Titian. NGL (Conzett & Huber) **133** "La Bella" by Titian. Pitti (Mella)—Ranuccio Farnese by Titian. NGAW, Kress—"Young Man in a Red Cap" by Lorenzo Lotto. Museo Correr (Giraudon) **134** "Abduction of the Body of St. Mark" by Tintoretto. Gallerie dell' Accademia (Eric Schaal, courtesy *Life*) **135** "The Crucifixion" by Tintoretto. Detail. Scuola di San Rocco (Eric Schaal, courtesy, *Life*) **136** "David" by Michelangelo. Detail. Galleria dell' Accademia, Florence **138** Aretino by Titian. The Frick Collection **141** Self-portrait by Alberti. NGAW, Kress **142** Castiglione by Raphael. Louvre (Giraudon) **145** Federigo da Montefeltro by Piero della Francesca. Uffizi **146** Spelling lesson. *El Modo da Insegnare Compitare*, Florence, *ca.* 1500 **147** Chess game. Jacapo de Cessolis, *Libro di Giuocho di Scacchi*, Florence, 1493 **148** Pius II. Codex 147, Biblioteca Corsini **149** Wood and stucco bust of a woman, 15th century. Anonymous. Louvre (*Realites*) **150** Gafori, *Theorica Musicae.* Milan, 1510. LC—Gafori, *Theorica Musicae.* Naples, 1480 **151** Pacioli by Jaco. . . Bar. . .Galleria Nazionale, Naples (Parisio) **152** Jupiter. Detail. *De Sphaera.* Ms. A.S. 2.14 BEM (Aldo Martello Editore)—Book presentation. Ms. CL. I 147, Libreria Ariosto, Ferrara **153** Fracastoro attributed to Torbido. NGL—Hospital. Ms. Gaddiano 24, BLF (ENIT) **154** Madonna by Fra Filippo Lippi. Pitti—Detail of Fra Filippo Lippi's tomb. Cathedral, Spoleto (Anderson) **155** Rospigliosi Cup by Cellini. MMA (Courtesy Shell Oil Company)—Study for "Perseus" by Cellini. MNF (Anderson)—Cellini by Vasari. Detail of "Cosimo I with Architects and Engineers." Palazzo Vecchio, Florence (Alinari) **156** Beatrice d'Este by Gian Cristoforo Romano. Isabella d'Este, drawing by Leonardo da Vinci. Both: Louvre (Giraudon) **157** Borso d' Este. *Genealogia Estense*, BEM—Francesco Gonzaga by Gian Cristoforo Romano, Museo Bardini, Florence (Alinari)—Lodovico Sforza. Cod. 2167, Biblioteca Trivulziana, Milan—Leonora of Aragon by Francesca Laurana. Galleria Nazionale, Palermo (G. Mannino) **158** Azay-le-Rideau (Spirale) **160** View of Arco by Dürer. Louvre (Giraudon) **161** "Surrender of Breda" by Velázquez. Prado, Madrid **162** Frances I by Clouet. Louvre (Giraudon) **163** Shakespeare. First folio, 1623. The Folger Shakespeare Library **164-165** Longleat by Jan Siberechts. Collection of the Marquess of Bath **166** "The Roman Forum" by Canaletto. By gracious permission of Her Majesty Queen Elizabeth, the Queen Mother.

INDEX

Page numbers in *italics* indicate illustrations. Individual works of art may be found by referring to the picture credits on page 167.